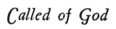

Called of God

Called of God:

THE WORK OF THE MINISTRY

GILBERT L. GUFFIN
Dean of Religion
Howard College
Formerly President,
The Eastern Baptist Theological Seminary

INTRODUCTION BY

ANDREW W. BLACKWOOD

THE CHRISTOPHER PUBLISHING HOUSE

BOSTON, U.S.A.

Library of Congress Catalog Card Number 65-26314

PRINTED IN THE UNITED STATES OF AMERICA

To
Lorene Parrish Guffin,
Faithful Helpmeet

CONTENTS

FOREWORD

This book is presented in the prayerful hope that it may be used to encourage the Christian ministry in this day. The author entertains the conviction that ministers are more responsible for the spiritual well-being of the world than any other group or class. The future, therefore, depends in large measure on the quality of the ministry of today.

After some years of close observation and study, and particularly in view of the fateful times through which the world is now passing, the writer is convinced that Christian preachers need to take heed to themselves and to their responsible task with awakened seriousness. He does not mean to presume he knows all the answers or that what is suggested in these chapters fully describes the ideal. His only hope is to make a contribution toward the encouragement, challenge, and strengthening of that body of people who are divinely commissioned not only to guide the world in the paths of rectitude but also to point the way to its salvation. To this end may God's grace rest on this humble effort.

A ministry that loses interest in its own enhancement will soon incur the judgment of both God and man. Although the ideal may never be attained, one must ever be pressing toward it. Both honesty and humility compel each of us to admit with Paul, "I do not consider myself to have 'arrived'"; but wisdom and revelation demand that we add, in the language of that same disciple, "But I keep going on, grasping ever more firmly that purpose for which Christ grasped me." * So

* Phil. 4:12-14. *Letters to Growing Churches,* J. B. Phillips.

may it be with every minister among us in this day of supreme challenge.

Too numerous are the authors, teachers, pastors and others who have influenced the writer in one way or another and contributed to his thinking with reference to the ministry for specific credit to be given here; but a word of appreciation should be expressed for the faithful work of my secretary, Miss Esther George, in the preparation of the manuscript; to Dr. J. O. Williams, Dr. John W. Bradbury, Dean Carl H. Morgan and Professors Ralph G. Turnbull and Robert G. Torbet, for the valuable suggestions each has made toward the refining processes necessary in the preparation of these chapters.

G. L. G.

INTRODUCTION

President Guffin holds up lofty ideals for the ministry. He bases everything on the Bible, in the light of history, with a view to the needs of today. He looks at the ministry as the noblest calling on earth, but only for the man whom the Lord counts worthy. Such a man appears on every page.

Unlike other idealists, Dr. Guffin concerns himself with ways and means. He believes in the best preparation for the ministry, and in the most efficient methods of doing God's work. Himself a conservative in doctrine, he welcomes the contributions of psychology, sociology, and anything else that makes the pastor aware of human needs, and able to meet them well.

With the book as a whole and in detail I agree heartily. I remember especially the folly of being an ecclesiastical clown, and the wisdom of choosing a wife able to become the leading woman in the community. Most of all do I endorse the parts about the minister himself as a man of God. With Woodrow Wilson I believe that this work consists mainly in being something, and that the power must come from God.

Every pastor needs such standards to test his ideals and practices. So does every student of theology. However zealous, a student ought often to check up, lest he become absorbed with means and lose sight of ends. Many a layman, also, instead of sitting in "the seat of the scornful," ought to "read, mark, learn and inwardly digest" such an account of the ministry, with all its ideals and difficulties.

In all these matters President Guffin himself affords an

object lesson. After years of preparation, culminating with an earned doctor's degree, he served well as pastor of local churches, so as to become doubly sure about the needs of the work today. Later at his home in the South he won laurels in a unique educational enterprise. Recently he became head of Eastern Baptist Seminary, where his spiritual vision and his educational program have already brought new life and strength to a young institution full of worth and promise.

What of this leader's hopes for the morrow? Judging from seminary students, I believe that the Church of tomorrow will have a ministerial leadership even more worthy than that of today. Never have I seen so many able young college and seminary graduates thronging our seminaries, and so many gifted professors striving to attain the ideals of this book. Hence I expect to witness a revival of concern about the local church as the most important institution in the world, except the home, and about the ministry as the noblest calling on earth.

Philadelphia, Pa.   ANDREW W. BLACKWOOD,
                                       Professor emeritus, Princeton
                                       Theological Seminary

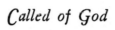

Called of God

1. The Minister and His Office

There has been a great deal of light talk with reference to the office of the minister. Even Christians, and sometimes ministers themselves, have condescended to speak disparagingly of it. A certain writer who apparently has a flair for making fun of the ministry remarked that he could not, for the life of him, see how any red-blooded man could stoop to be a minister.

Someone has said, rather contemptuously it would appear, that there are three sexes, masculine, feminine, and ministers.

At a large community gathering in one of our Eastern states the writer heard the following story which about sums up the opinion of a great mass of people of this day regarding the minister:

A salesman met a minister in a hotel one day and engaged the minister in a conversation. The salesman, not knowing the minister, asked, "What is your business? Are you a salesman, too?"

"Yes," replied the minister, "I am a salesman."

"What is your line?" asked the salesman.

"Why, I sell the most important thing in the world," the minister replied.

The salesman said, "Could that be dry goods?"

The minister shook his head.

"Groceries?" asked the salesman.

"No, not groceries."

"Well, then, is it armaments?"

"No."

"Well," replied the salesman, somewhat perplexed, "it must be notions."

"Some people think it is," said the minister. "You see, I am a preacher."

Peddlers of notions! That, unfortunately, is about the height of the conception some people hold regarding the work of the ministry.

I

How important, then, is the work of the ministry? Let the greatest preacher since Christ answer. "I magnify my office," he makes bold to say. This is no endeavor on Paul's part to magnify himself. Far from it. Concerning himself he feels compelled to say, "I am the least of all the apostles, who am not worthy to be called an apostle." Certainly, he would turn no eye of favor on himself, but he did want the Romans, at the center of the world of that day, and men everywhere, to know the importance of the Christian ministry. So he writes, "I lay great stress on my office. I put great store by it. I glorify my ministry." Paul had no desire to glorify himself, but he would allow no one to think or speak lightly of his office.

No one can deny the fact that the New Testament puts the office of the ministry first in responsibility, if not in importance, in Christian service. "For after that in the wisdom of God the world by wisdom knew not God, it pleased God by the foolishness of preaching to save them that believe." *

Preaching is a pivotal part of God's chosen way of turning the world unto Himself. He has numerous other ways, but this one is at the center. Through the "foolishness" ** of what we preach it pleased God to turn to Himself a world that in its own wisdom had failed to find God.

The emphasis in this statement, to be sure, is not on the art of preaching but on the subject matter preached, namely, the Cross or the significance of the Redemptive work of Christ having its center at Golgotha. This, one should note in passing, suggests a whole theological education in a nutshell, so significant that, to take it seriously, would revise the direction presently taken by some theological institutions which by avoiding the Cross have missed their way.

Even though the major emphasis of the present text is admittedly on the thing preached and not on preaching itself, still the thought of the apostle is clearly reflective of his conviction that the burden of conveying this mes-

* I Cor. 1:21.
** A more accurate translation is: "the foolishness of *the* preaching." The reference is to the thing preached, and not to the act of preaching. See The American Standard Revision.

sage of the Cross to the world which, through its own wisdom has been unable to find the way, rests chiefly upon the preacher. His choice of the term "preaching" suggests as much.

Such is obviously true also of the phrase in Romans 10:14, "How shall they hear *without a preacher?*" The following verse used by the apostle in this connection makes clear what Paul means, for he goes on to say, "How shall they preach, except they be sent? as it is written, How beautiful are the feet of them that preach the gospel of peace, and bring glad tidings of good things!"

The fact pointed up here gives distinction to the office of the ministry. Well may one afford to magnify this office when he senses the importance God has given it. This alone would demand that the utmost in appreciation, consecration and determination be given to it by those who are called to its high position.

There are other reasons, moreover, for magnifying the office of the ministry. *The scope of its responsibility emphasizes its importance.*

II

What is the responsibility of the office of the ministry? First, it is in part that of *intermediary* between the people and God. The minister, no matter what his denominational affiliation, performs in this sense, but in this sense only, the work of a priest. He stands between the people he serves and their God in a unique way, and continually

THE MINISTER AND HIS OFFICE

bears the burden of their spiritual welfare up to the throne
of God. Like the priest of old, he intercedes for the people
and represents them at the altar of mercy. This function
is fulfilled, not by the clothing one wears, or the para-
phernalia one uses, but by the service one renders. Of
course, all Christians are "kings and priests" * before God
and may and must go directly to God for pardon and
help; and every individual is fully accountable for his be-
liefs and behavior, whether he be layman or minister.
The distinction between the layman and the minister at
this point is not so much in the nature of the work of
intercession but in the greater degree in which it is done
by the minister. The true minister of the Gospel, like
Paul, always has the people "in his heart" and is ever burdened for their spiritual health. In this sense and because
of this fact, he represents the people before God in a way
similar to Aaron's ministry in Israel.

The office of the minister is also the office of *prophet.*
In this capacity he represents God to the people. God has
especially chosen the ministry as His channel through
which to proclaim His message to the people. Every true
minister is a prophet. This does not mean that he is
primarily a foreteller. The word "prophet," in its original
sense, means a *forthteller,* not a *foreteller.* The prophet
is one who speaks God's message for Him. The message
may include prediction, but it also includes much more.
It is not the nature of the message but the fact that one

* Rev. 1:6. (In I Peter 2:9 "a royal priesthood" carries the
same idea.)

delivers God's message that makes him a prophet. The minister is a prophet who hears the Word of the Lord and speaks for God. This places high responsibility, then, on his office. With what humility, with what utter consecration one ought to give himself to prayer and meditation, that, through communion with God, he may be certain that he speaks for God! Wherever a minister fails in this definitely appointed responsibility, he does so to his own hurt, to the dishonor of his Lord, to the discredit of the ministry and to the delusion of the people.

The office of the ministry is, moreover, that of *guide* or *example* to the people. One cannot magnify the responsibility of his office too greatly at this point. Justly may the minister be censured and the people pitied when there is a failure here. If the blind lead the blind they shall both fall into the ditch. Let every minister strive so to live that he may be able to say with Paul, "Follow me," and know at the same time that the people will be following Christ as they follow him.

The office of the minister should be magnified, furthermore, because it is *charged with* the responsibility of *teaching truth* of destiny-determining importance. By virtue of the position of the minister in the plan of Christ, he is more responsible than any other for fulfilling the third part of the Great Commission, "teaching them to observe all things whatsoever I have commanded you." The minister who is faithful to his office is constantly teaching. He does so not only in Sunday-school classes, leadership courses, and other groups that he may be asked to instruct,

but he does it also in his preaching, in his calls at the
home, in conversation, interviews and conferences he may
hold in his study or elsewhere. He keeps ever before him
his responsibility, and uses every opportunity to fulfill it.
He is never released from his obligation to correct error,
to enlighten men concerning the Truth and to help men
understand the message of the Scriptures. Of this fact
every sincere minister is constantly aware. How great
stress must be laid upon an office which carries such a
responsibility! The Christian Church is doomed to peril-
ous weakness and the world to disaster if those who have
been called to the office of the ministry fail here. The
office demands an able, consecrated, enlightened service
of teaching.

The office of the ministry carries also the task of being
soul-physician to the people. Higher qualifications were
never more needed for the doctor who ministers to the
bodies of men than for the one who ministers to the souls
of men. One must be an able diagnostician if he diag-
noses the spiritual malady of every soul for whom he is
responsible. He needs also to know how, having diag-
nosed the condition, to point out, and if needs be to apply,
the remedy.

There is fortunately a growing awareness among us of
the values inherent in the right kind of personal counseling. The wide-awake minister will take proper advantage of the help available to him in these times to enable
him to become an increasingly effective counselor. The
work of a true physician of souls is not confined simply

to those who may come to him for counsel. He will seek out the mentally, socially, and spiritually sick, that he may minister to their needs even before they may be aware of these needs themselves. "Pastoral Counseling" is a modern term, but the service it connotes has been a never-ending duty. To be sure, good shepherds of the flock actually have, through all the centuries, been doing the work of personal counseling without any knowledge of the modern term for it. However, this fact does not excuse the minister of today from his obligation to take fullest advantage of the information as to techniques and guidance now available for those who would do a successful work in this field.

Two cautions are in order at this point: (1) One should not feel he must confine his counseling to an office procedure nor that he should seek recognition officially as a personal counselor. The highest honor possible is that of a "good minister of Jesus Christ." A more effective ministry in counseling can be performed with this title than with any other title conceivable. (2) Do not try to be a psychiatrist. This is the work of a specialist. Every case not solvable by personal counseling, including prayer, the use of the Scriptures and of spiritual guidance, should be referred to a psychiatrist as promptly as possible. One should take care, however, to refer the patient to a Christian psychiatrist. It is far more important from the patient's standpoint that this psychiatrist be a Christian than that his physician be one.

The office of the ministry is charged with *pastoral*

responsibility. No matter how myriad his other duties may be, the minister ought to remember that one of his most important tasks is to be a real pastor. He must lead and guide and comfort and care for the people as a shepherd who will lay down his life for the sheep. Surely the flock of God never needed genuine pastoral work more than in this hour. The mass of the broken-hearted and confused, fearful and tension-laden, and the increasing numbers who turn to the psychiatrists are convincing evidences of this fact. Every true minister will lay great stress on his work of being a real pastor. The one aspect of pastoral work, comforting the people, is a Herculean task in itself. With sorrow, terror and death on every hand, God is still saying to His prophets, "Comfort ye, comfort ye my people. Speak ye comfortingly unto my people." It is not surprising that near the end of his career, Ian MacLaren of Glasgow said that if he could live his life over again he would preach more comfortingly to the people. The minister who neglects to comfort those who need comfort has forsaken one of the highest obligations of his office; but the one who comforts the people both glorifies his ministry and gladdens the heart of God.

The office of the minister not only obligates one to be an intermediary, a prophet, a guide, a teacher, a soul-physician, and a pastor, but it also demands that one be a *servant.* The immortal Paul said, "We preach not ourselves unto you, but we preach Jesus Christ, and ourselves your servants." This must ever be the ideal and practice of the ministry if it is to be true to its office. The minister, although he need not be a bellhop or an errand boy, ought to be the chief servant of all, ministering to the church, the poor, the friendless, to the community and beyond the community, wherever he may serve in the name of his Master.

But the crowning work of the ministry is that of *evangelization*. This is the highest responsibility of the office. The minister is charged to do the work of an evangelist. There is no excuse for us and little hope for the church and the world if we fail in this obligation. Of course, evangelism is not the responsibility of ministers exclusively —it belongs to every person who names the Name of Christ—but the minister must ever be an example in soul-winning and ought to be the chief soul-winner among the people. From this task there can be no release, nor can there ever be a legitimate answer for its neglect. Let no minister ever forget that:

> The despairing cry of dying men,
> Under the curse of their mortal sin,
> The verdict of the ages,
> The command of the Skies,
> Is Evangelize! Evangelize!

The highest office to which a minister may attain ecclesiastically or otherwise is insignificant compared to the accomplishment of leading one soul to Christ. The minister cannot satisfy his responsibility simply by teaching and training others to win souls. When a preacher loses his passion for souls the pulpit freezes over, the people get frostbite in the pew and a death-dealing glacier develops in the community. No matter what else the minister does, nothing can become an adequate substitute for his winning souls to Christ. Under no circumstance may he properly excuse himself from this responsibility. Every minister who weighs rightly the obligation of his office will pray:

> "Give me a voice, a cry and a complaining,
> Oh, let my sound be stormy in their ears!
> Throat that would shout, but cannot stay for straining;
> Eyes that would weep, but cannot wait for tears.
> Quick! In a moment, infinite forever!
> Send an arousal better than I pray!
> Give me a grace upon my faint endeavor!
> Souls for my hire, and Pentecost today!" *

What has been said above expresses, at least in part, something of the scope of the responsibility of the office of the Christian ministry. When it is remembered that eternal consequences hang upon almost every utterance and act of the minister, then who can overstate the responsibility of his office? Every sentence expressed from the pulpit or in personal guidance may be—possibly always is—freighted with weal or woe to some soul; every word may be the savor of life unto life or of death unto death for someone. The words of no other person in any other office carry such eternal consequences. While the words

* F. W. W. Myers, *St. Paul, Collected Poems*, Macmillan Company.

of the physician, the lawyer, the scientist, or the statesman concern matters which, at best, are of only temporal importance, the words of the minister concern matters of eternal destiny. Probably no one ever hears a sermon without being made better or worse. It is unlikely that one is ever the same afterward. He is either hardened or helped, made more callous or more consecrated, becomes more resistant to the voice of the Holy Spirit or more ready to heed the will of the Lord. How tremendously important, then, is the office concerned with such weighty eventualities.

III

The office of the Christian ministry ought to be magnified because God placed it first in importance in the work of His Kingdom on earth and also because of the great scope of its responsibility. But there is a third reason why it should be magnified, namely, *the nature of its requirements.*

No other office on earth carries with it such weighty requirements as does that of the Christian ministry. Few people outside of the ministry and probably not all within the office know and appreciate the requirements laid upon a minister in this day. All are agreed that a minister must be a good man and highly regarded in his community. But what further requirements rest upon him?

What are the requirements of the minister educationally? At least in this day, if, indeed, it was ever otherwise, the minister needs to be one of the best informed men in his parish. The educational opportunities for a minister rank well with those for any other profession. This statement may be doubted, but an investigation will prove its validity. To earn the top degree in theology in a standard seminary requires, above the A.B. degree or its equivalent, a minimum of six years of study and research. It is neither necessary nor possible for every minister to earn a doctor's degree, but the level of training among the people he serves and the exalted nature of his work make a combined and compelling reason that every minister obtain the best training possible.

As to the range of the subjects required in the well prepared minister's curriculum, they may be summarized as follows: (a) The Bible—a study of its background, source, languages, interpretation; (b) Church Administration, including the technique of leadership, the training of leaders, the organizations of the church and the methods of efficiently operating them, and scores of other matters affecting the work of the church; (c) Homiletics, or the art of preaching; (d) Psychology; (e) Philosophy; (f) Christian Education; (g) Sociology; (h) Church History; (i) Christian Doctrine, including the history of doctrine as well as Biblical theology; (j) Anthropology; (k) Evangelism and Missions; (l) Music and Worship techniques; (m) Pastoral Ministries and Personal Counseling; (n) Comparative Religion, or an understanding of the religions of man; (o) Archæology. To this list other specialties may be added, such as a study of the rural church, pastoral problems, literature, and clinical training. Although any theological school would probably admit that its curriculum is not perfect, it must be agreed that the average seminary curriculum affords an extensive educational experience.

What are the requirements of the office of the minister in business ability? The average person does not grant that a minister ordinarily has qualifications in a business way. This is probably the result of the fact that ministers usually do not engage in secular business, nor do they often accumulate a fortune. But it is a fact that to be a successful minister in this day one must be highly gifted in business ability. To be able to guide and advise the modern church in its extensive organization and program demands great acumen. It has been amazing to the present writer to see how helpless a group of business executives can be with the problems of their church. He has seen men of considerable success as officials in great business concerns who would go about the work of their church in deplorably unbusinesslike ways. To be sure, the reason for this may have been that many business men do not take time or have sufficient interest to apply their business ability to the work of the church; but this very fact makes it all the more necessary that the pastor possess the business ability needed to lead the church successfully. Usually it is the task of the pastor to see to it that the work of the church, even including the financial program, is carried on in a businesslike fashion.

The business ability required of the minister is also

demonstrated in his personal affairs. Ministers generally live on a notoriously low salary. Yet they must live on a social level in keeping with the better class of those whom they serve. They must dress presentably. They must furnish their homes properly. They are expected to contribute to every good cause. They must set the pace for giving in their churches and almost always give more heavily in proportion to ability than anybody else in their churches. Besides all this, they usually manage to send their children to college and also to carry a fairly heavy load of insurance as their chief means of security in illness and old age.

To these evidences of the business ability of the minister may be added the fact that ministers' sons seem better prepared than others to become wealthy, presumably because of frugality, economy, and other tendencies that have been cultivated in them from childhood, and certainly not because of inheritance. In a grouping of the wealthiest men in the country a few years ago one-third of them were discovered to be ministers' sons Of course, it may be contended that it is resentment over weariness with the straitened circumstances of their childhood or else a desire of more than usual power to gain riches engendered by these same circumstances which has caused ministers' sons to make such a notable record. Although this may have been true in some cases, it seems an inadequate explanation for the exceptional record made by children of the parsonage.

Even if it be assumed that the sons of ministers would

possess business ability, their number is far out of proportion to their ratio as a class. It simply points to the fact *that successful ministers do and must* have business ability. The exigencies of their lives force them almost more than anybody else to learn how to make a dollar go farther and accomplish more. Admittedly, the minister's wife must be given her part of the credit, and at times, perhaps, the larger part of it, for their record. This fact, however, does not change the truth of the point under discussion. It is only a part of the answer.

The office of the minister demands executive ability. The success of a minister depends in a large degree on how good an executive he is. In a secular business an executive can get things done through the power of his position and the desire of employes to hold their jobs. The head of a school can get things done because of the authority he holds. But a minister can use neither of these levers. He is cast back almost entirely on his innate executive ability. The church in this day has become an intricate organization. Looked at from the material point of view, it is an amazingly complicated piece of machinery. Woe to the minister who is not a good engineer, able to keep all the parts functioning properly and in orderly relationship. Knowing that no worker is moved by the salary motive or the fear-of-discipline motive, the minister can legitimately use only good judgment and strong appeal as his means of keeping things going. He must depend on tact and diplomacy, but these must always be unmixed with deceit or with compromise of a principle.

Unexpected as it may be in Christians, many of them—some holding places of outstanding leadership—must be handled constantly with "kid gloves." Dr. Austen K. de Blois has put it graphically in the following lines:

We meet with the brother who scolds and the sister who gossips; the prim and the formal folks; the strait-laced and the over-pious souls who are unctuously desirous that all other souls shall be as flagrantly pious as they suppose themselves to be; the dyspeptic pessimist who bewails the fact that the church is not what it used to be, and the gushing optimist who looks upon the pastor as an improved edition of Brooks plus Spurgeon, and the choir as an aggregation of angels; the small-sized man who wants to see the church run on an efficient and businesslike basis; the deacon who laments the decline of Pentecostal power and the trustee who wants the boys' club shut down because the young imps have broken three chairs and smashed a window; the gentleman who appears on Easter Sunday, compliments the pastor, praises the church, replies to the admiring coterie of friends who surge about him that he intends to come now every Sunday, regularly, "yes, indeed," and then disappears again until next Easter; the critics, the boasters, the slackers; the dominant ones, the timid ones, the nervous ones; the splenetic, the fanatic, the erratic; the pompous usher, the anxious treasurer, the meticulous church clerk, the Sunday-school teacher who cannot teach and the young people's leader who cannot lead; the singer with an everlasting chip on his shoulder and the sexton who never pleases anybody.*

* Austen K. de Blois, *Some Problems of the Modern Minister,* Sunday School Board, Southern Baptist Convention, 1928, p. 248.

With all the above types and personalities the pastor must get along, as well as cause them to get along agreeably among themselves, and he must do it all by persuasion, tact and love. He cannot do it by force or by fear.

Not only does the office of minister make high demands on one in education, business and executive ability, but *it also requires that one literally give himself as upon an altar of sacrifice in faithful endeavor and hard work*. The demands on his time and energy are almost unceasing. There is no room for one who is lazy or indolent. He has no "hours"; all his time is at public demand.

Others may refuse to go on call, but the minister cannot. No matter how much one does, there is always much more to be done. The average successful minister, especially in the town and city pastorates, spends twelve to sixteen and more hours a day at work. If it were not for the variation afforded in his work he could not endure the strain.

A few years ago the writer ran across a survey of professional men somebody had made. The essence of it, as he recalls, was that the minister prepares enough messages in a year to constitute a large three-volume work, which equals the output of the best writers. He may have as many personal interviews as the average lawyer. He does more study than the average schoolteacher. It is necessary for him to read as many books as the average librarian. He has about as many conferences and committee meetings as the average official. And all of this constitutes only a part of his activities! Though this survey clearly concerns the work of the more outstanding pastors of the larger churches, the worthy pastor in any field has a full-time job. Yet there are many people, even in the church, who think all a minister has to do is to preach once or twice on Sunday and perhaps conduct prayer-meeting during the week. The critic who said he did not see, for the life of him, how any red-blooded man could consent to become a minister and twiddle his life away in comparative idleness and worthlessness revealed nothing but his own tragic ignorance of the facts, or the bad example of some ministers. Then some people wonder what a preacher does with his time between Sundays when they think that all he may do is to conduct a mid-week prayer meeting!

Furthermore, *the office of minister requires a high level of consecration.* There can be no compromise or lowering of the standards. A minister *must* walk with his Lord. He *must* manifest a godly life. The obligations on him are rigid and tremendous. If others fail to see Christ in him, his voice will be empty, and those who follow him may be misled. If he stumbles morally nobody can measure the greatness of the hurt. All his fellow ministers suffer. People outside of the church are hardened and are made more difficult to win. It is a calamity of the first magnitude. The public may forgive anyone else for a "slip," but not a minister. One misstep and he is ruined. News occasionally reaches the public of the tragedy that has come to some church in the form of a charge of moral misconduct against its pastor. A shadow is always cast over all the churches in any area when this happens, and every minister shares the hurt.

The office of the ministry requires, moreover, that one be selfless in his attitude and service. His motive, as is true of every Christian, though probably not in the same degree, must be for others' good and not for personal gain. His service must be rendered for the blessing of others and the glory of God, but never for self aggrandizement. He should live above offense. No matter what people do or say, no matter how much they try to hurt, no matter how thoughtless or willful or cold, the minister is expected to remain even-tempered and never to show that he is offended or hurt. Though one may long ever so much for sympathy and often fail to receive it from the people, he must never forget to be sympathetic. Forgetting himself, the good minister stands beside every soul, whether the condition of that soul be one of need, distress, persecution, disappointment or sorrow, and understandingly helps that soul to bear its load.

Finally, *the office of the ministry requires the utmost in sacrifice.* "When we cease to bleed," said J. H. Jowett, one of the truly great preachers of the past generation, "we cease to bless." No more profound warning than this was ever given to ministers. Jesus reminded His disciples that a servant is not above his Lord. For Him the *via dolorosa* lay between Himself and man's completed salvation. Can His servants expect less? From first to last, the minister who truly magnifies his office is required to be an example in sacrificial living.

Dr. B. H. Carroll, distinguished Baptist preacher and educator, spoke a word of profound truth when he said, "I maintain that there is no other office known among men that calls for the kind and degree of qualifications which God's Word requires for the ministerial office. The minister must have gifts, graces and character such as no human law requires for any earthly office."

"I magnify my office," says Paul. "I put great store by it. I lay great stress upon it." Let this be the purpose and practice of all ministers of the Gospel of Christ!

An adequate ministry *will* "magnify" its office.

> Not on the gory field of fame
>   Their noble deeds were done;
> Not in the sound of earth's acclaim
>   Their fadeless crowns were won.
> Not from the palaces of kings,
>   Nor fortune's sunny clime,
> Came the great souls, whose life-work flings
>   Luster o'er earth and time.
>
> For truth with tireless zeal they sought;
>   In joyless paths they trod—
> Heedless of praise or blame, they wrought,
>   And left the rest to God.
> The lowliest sphere was not disdained;
>   Where love could soothe or save,
> They went, by fearless faith sustained,
>   Nor knew their deeds were brave.*
>   —EDWARD HARTLEY DEWART.

* "God's Heroes," in *Poems With Power To Strengthen The Soul*, compiled by James Mudge, The Abingdon Press.

2. The Minister and His Task

Pastoral work, teaching, preaching, and evangelism are all Scriptural requirements and practical necessities. It is imperative that they be given their proper place in the colossal program which the Master committed to His followers. When this has been said, however, there is yet room for a more complete and inclusive statement of that which must constitute the objective of the ministry which is to be effective in "such a time as this."

If our ministry is to be comparable to that of apostolic times and if it is to meet successfully the poignant needs of this hour, it *must* be an all-inclusive or comprehensive ministry. This means that our ministry shall not only include and harmonize in proper proportions the pastoral, the teaching, the preaching and the evangelistic functions, but that it shall also be complete in its preparation, its outlook, its method and its use of resources.

I

The ministry for such a time as this must be *comprehensive in preparation*. In a word, such preparation requires that the ministry shall be ready in heart, in spirit, in the sense of its divine call, and in the quality and extent of its scholastic training.

For the ministry to be ready in heart means that each minister by personal surrender, dedication and faith, must have made Christ both Saviour and Lord of his life. It implies all that the New Testament teaches as to the manner in which one becomes a follower of the Master. Were it not for the fact that readiness of heart is imperative, not merely for every minister but for every one who would name His Name, it would seem elementary and trite to mention it in this connection. Jesus was speaking about the condition of the heart, not about the lack of knowledge, when He said, "And if the blind lead the blind, both shall fall into the ditch." Calamity, dissolution and despair will be the inevitable results if the spiritually blind guide the blind.

All too frequently the necessity for preparation in spirit has been overlooked. When the minister's disposition— the quality of his temper and mental attitudes—is such that it repels those whom he ought to win, the results may be tragic. Bitterness, vindictiveness, unrestrained temper, coldness, and disagreeableness have no more place in a minister's personality than do weakness, absence of convictions, lack of positiveness, and effeminacy. The Psalmist's prayer should constantly be on the minister's lips, "Renew a right spirit within me." It is as true for the minister as for anyone else that "they who have not the spirit of Christ are none of his."

Of vital importance to a comprehensive preparation for the ministry is the fact that it shall have a deep and abiding sense of its *divine call*. That ministry which has not a profound assurance of the divine urge within it is doomed in the course of time to lose its sense of urgency and possibly to come to failure. When God's prophets speak and labor under an undoubted conviction of their heaven-given commission to speak His message in His Name, they will be indomitable and their message commanding and dynamic.

Man-called or "mother-called" preachers, as the case may be, are likely to come to disillusionment and at best their work will lack the punch and drive of those who are under the spell of a sense of high mission and imperious orders. Many of those who have no sense of call fade out of the ministry or merely drift with the tide. The sense of call and mission, burningly and inescapably urging one onward, seems imperative for a ministry competent to match itself with the current tide of iniquity and world-wide anguish.

On the other hand, it appears that some of those who ought to enter the ministry succeed in resisting, at whatever price, the divine urge laid upon them. Low salaries, intensified demands on the minister, the growing influence of secularism and the total pattern of modern life have combined to make it difficult for a young man to surrender to the call of the ministry. Yet men of the finest intellect and background are increasingly needed for this highest of all callings.

Although it is recognized that God can take ordinary men and through them do extraordinary work, it is equally true that when He wants to do the work of a

Moses or an Elijah or a Paul, He calls men of towering natural ability and intellect. Somehow, the day must be recaptured when young men of this caliber will not turn away from the ministry but enlarging numbers of them be moved to answer the divine summons, "Whom shall I send, and who will go for us?" with Isaiah's response, "Here am I, Lord; send me."

This call may come in varied forms and many factors may enter into it, but the conviction need be none the less compulsive. When one becomes convinced within that the will of God requires his full surrender to the work of the ministry he will have no alternative but to obey.

Of course, another phase of preparation which the ministry dare not neglect in such a time as this is that of scholastic training. This age demands scholarship of the minister. To ignore this fact is to do so at one's peril. It is expected that the ministry shall be learned not only in its particular field, but also in the general field of education. Doubtless the minister's position calls for a wider learning than do many others in which men engage. However, this general culture should not be taken as sufficient for the good minister of Christ. His knowledge of his own field should be broad and deep. He must know more about it than any lay member of his church. In a word, he needs to be a specialist. To do so, he requires more than merely a college and seminary education. One must be both a perennial and a persistent student, constantly uniting his knowledge with his experience and

making them practical for the needs to which he ministers.

II

The ministry for such a time as this must be *comprehensive* in *outlook*. This outlook should include, first of
all, the Church, with all its immediate needs. Diligent, persistent study should be given to knowing the weaknesses
and imperfections of the church, its problems and responsibilities, its organizations and their processes, its importance in and impact on the world. Each minister should
examine the church of which he is the under-shepherd to
know the measure in which it conforms to the New Testament standard. Then, carefully, prayerfully and coura-
geously, he should lead it to the realization of that
standard. Most evangelical Christians have gloried in the
great basic doctrine of the recognition of the New Testament as the sole and sufficient rule of faith and practice.
When the Christian ministry ceases to be concerned about
leading the churches for which it is responsible to the attainment of the New Testament standard, it will have
automatically and indelibly written "Ichabod" over its
threshold, and the doom of that ministry will be the
despair of the world.

The outlook of the comprehensive ministry not only
includes the Church with its many needs, but it also em-
braces the world with all its problems and perplexities.
The Church is not simply an organization affording a

position, or even a field for service, but it is a home base and the whole world the field—the great mission field for which we are responsible. The supreme problem of the world and the genesis of every other problem is sin; the greatest need man has ever seen is that of a personal Saviour from sin.

> Come, ye disconsolate, where'er ye languish;
> Come to the mercy-seat, fervently kneel;
> Here bring your wounded hearts, here tell your anguish.
> Earth has no sorrow that Heaven cannot heal.

Recognizing the value of a personality made in the image of God to be greater than the value of a world, we must endeavor to bring each individual into personal union with Christ, in whom alone he can realize all the possibilities for which he was created.

But inseparably related to the world's need for a personal Saviour from sin is the world's need for universal deliverance from sin's enthraldom. Men are fettered to systems and conditions which are dragging their very souls into destruction. The ministry which is truly comprehensive in outlook places itself in the midst of such shackled humanity and, refusing to relent or compromise, wields its utmost strength to free the enslaved. The ears of the multitudes of forlorn, hungry, oppressed, and degenerate men will be deaf to the Gospel message so long as those who deliver the message play friends to the influences, powers and systems, responsible for their condition, and manifest no interest in their plight. Taking on its lips the message of personal redemption from sin and in its heart a sympathetic understanding of the life-destroying problems and perplexities of humankind, the ministry comprehensive in outreach must thrust itself out into the world in which men really live, must love them, and must help them fight their battles against sin.

To be specific, the problem of hungry masses of people is a matter of concern for us even if these people do live in a conquered or foreign land. Sin is somehow to blame for this condition. It is our task to fight sin wherever it dares to show its hideous presence. Then the causes back of this human tragedy must have our concern. He would be a foolish physician who would attempt to treat a cancer by simply applying a poultice to the affected external tissue. A wise physician would attempt to get at the roots of the cancer. He would not stop until he had done all in his power to extract every semblance of the deadly growth from the body of the patient. Likewise, must we get back to the root causes for the world's problems and exert our utmost to correct them at their sources.

It is not enough to feed the hungry, salvage the drunkard, or rescue the child orphaned by divorce; we must try to change the conditions which bring about the tragedies. When heartless corporations or men of ungodly business practices take advantage of employes, or employes become careless regarding their moral obligation to give full returns in labor for wages received, it is our responsibility to try to see that justice and right prevail.

If subtle, selfish interests are willing to pay the price of

others' blood that they may prosper; if they are engaged
in forcing the world to commit suicide that they may
have their little mess of pottage, it will be to the perpetual
shame of God's prophets to sit idly by without a word of
challenge or of condemnation. If in a world where defiant
atheism, backed by great political powers, and subtle ma-
terialism threaten to destroy men's faith in God and to
uproot all moral principles from society, then the pulpit
that is awake will sound the clarion call of the Gospel
and proclaim the certainty of divine judgment as never
before. If in a world reeking with corruption and crime
the ministry is satisfied with cavilings and prattle, then
it must be prepared to accept without complaint the
anathema of the ages.

If atheistic communism with fanatical zeal and fiendish
subtlety, casting overboard every moral consideration that
does not appear to serve its own interests, threatens to
enslave the world and attempts to drive Christianity with
all other religions from the earth, the minister is blind
who does not recognize that an hour of fate is upon us,
that he is confronted with the challenge of an antichrist,
and that his utmost is demanded for the emergency. If
secularism moves like a poisonous pall across the earth,
even in many cases casting its shadows across the cam-
puses of once notably Christian schools and seeping into
our homes and suffocating the Christian emphasis on
public education, then the ministry that is awake must
sound the alarm.

The souls of men and possibly the destiny of nations

and civilization are at stake. It is God who has made us our brother's keepers, and it is to Him that we are responsible for our stewardship.

Almighty God, how we forget
　　Thy vengeance on the guilty Cain!
We dream the dream of envy yet,
　　And brother is by brother slain.

Shall memory hold to greed and crime
　　And all the wrongs that sin hath bred,
Nor light her torch with love sublime
　　By heaven through the ages shed?

O Star that shone on Judæa's hill!
　　Lead, kindly Light; we'll follow thee;
Though hate's dark cloud breaks on us still
　　The dream of love that's yet to be.*

III

The ministry for today must be *comprehensive in method.* Is there not among ministers of the present age, despite all our learning and advance along other lines, a woeful incompleteness and inadequacy concerning this tremendously important matter? We have hardly begun, it seems, to make use of the great avenues for service which are afforded us in Christ. Sadly must we admit that all too frequently we have adopted one or two methods, and have stumbled blindly over the many others which have been lying in our very pathway. We

* Ernest Neal, *A Second Book of Verse* (Macon, Ga.: The J. W. Burks Printing Co., 1928), p. 129.

have too often been but hobby riders and slaves of tradition and habit, when we ought to have been trail blazers.

This is a plea for nothing off-color, strange or fantastic. It is simply a plea that we study anew the life and ministry of our Lord in order to discover the methods He used to reach the hearts of men. Let it be said with emphasis: every method which Jesus utilized we may legitimately and wisely, yea, we must, employ. If He first lived out that which He intended to teach, thus preparing the hearts of people to hear, we do well to tarry long with Him to learn His method. If He made Himself so winsome and lovable that He was a welcomed guest even at the nuptial occasion of the village swain of Cana, is it not time for us to learn the potential power of winsomeness and lovableness? If Jesus first ministered to the physical needs of the multitudes that He might more effectively minister to their spiritual needs, is it too much that the servants shall be as their Lord? If Jesus so lived and labored that the oppressed multitudes recognized Him as a friend, as One who loved, sympathized with and understood them, surely it is incumbent on us that we so live and labor that similar multitudes of today will recognize our likeness to our Master. If in Jesus all castes met on a common ground, then it behooves His ministers to know no low or high degree, but to lift all alike to the higher common level of brotherhood in Christ.

If Jesus in His sinlessness counted Himself not too good to sit at meat with publicans and sinners that He might break to them the Bread of Life, surely His ministers will count no man too wretchedly sinful or unworthy for us to place our hearts alongside his heart and love him into the Kingdom. We may rejoice that the ministry of these times does commend itself well in this respect. If Jesus took His message out into the city streets and the country lanes where the people really were, is it not obligatory on us to do likewise? Rather, has not the hour struck when we must follow His example or face consequences too grim and awful to contemplate? The masses are not coming to church today. If they are to be reached, the church must go to them. If the Son of God was never too busy or tired, even in the heat of the midday or the darkness of the midnight, to speak to individuals about things of eternal importance, and to preach to them the message of life, then surely we will never have really begun to give the proper place and importance to the function of personal evangelization until we are willing to do the same.

IV

If the Christian ministry would be truly adequate for such a time as this, it must be not only comprehensive in preparation, in outlook and in method, but it *must also be comprehensive in resources*. In other words, it must lay hold of its unlimited, and, in this age, almost untapped sources of power. I shall name only the two major resources available.

The first, and one which certainly we could greatly strengthen, are the resources which would accrue from the living of more truly victorious lives of sacrificial service on the part of the ministry. By victorious lives is meant lives unspotted and undefeated by sin and the harmful practices of the world; lives lived in the world, yet lives which have become by no means a part of the world. Too few of us dare or even seem to care to be saints. By lives of sacrificial service is meant lives which have been placed without any reservation on the altar for Christ's sake and the Gospel's, lives which have been given to the cause in His name and for the sake of others without any counting of the cost, lives of humble, courageous, persistent obedience to the Master's command.

Never will the ministry of this or any other day become imperative until those who preach the Word first live that which they preach. It is only when Christians live as the Master taught them to live that the world to any appreciable degree gives heed to the Church and its message. In this matter of right living it is imperative that the ministry lead the way. "It is of no use to walk anywhere to preach," said a great Christian long ago, "unless we preach as we walk."

The only legitimate and real authority which the true Christian ministry possesses rests in and is measured by its sacrificial service. That ministry which is not given in loving, sacrificial service is forfeiting its right to both influence and authority. On the other hand, that ministry which is giving itself in real sacrificial service is wielding almost immeasurable influence and authority.

Second, divine aid, as every true minister well knows,

is imperative. To the thoughtful person the requirements essential for an effective ministry no doubt seem difficult or impossible of attainment. This is granted. In fact, these requirements are impossible of fulfillment without Divine aid. We may rejoice and take courage, however, that the resources of God the Father, Son and Holy Spirit are unlimited and eternal. And these resources may be ours, yea, God invites us to have them, if we will but lay hold on them in the proper way. By obedience, by prayer, by faith, by consecration, by opening our hearts to Him, by surrendering to Him every faculty we possess we will be clothed with power limited only by the limits of His purposes for our lives.

What Spurgeon aptly said to the Church, the faithful Christian ministry would do well to take to heart:

> O Church of God! believe thyself invincible, and thou art invincible; but stay to tremble and fear, and thou art undone. Lift up thy head and say, "I am God's daughter; I am Christ's bride." Do not stop to prove it, but affirm it; march through the land, and kings and princes shall bow down before thee, because thou hast taken thine ancient prowess and assumed thine ancient glory.

When the infinite resources of the Triune God, whom we serve and whose we are, have been joined with the consecrated resources of victorious lives of sacrificial service, then and only then shall we begin to see the kingdom of God prevail on earth in a manner worthy of His Name.

O Father, grant Thy love divine
To make these mystic temples thine.

3. The Minister and His Motive

Is the minister's motive adequate for these times? We need to be sure. Perhaps a re-examination of the motives which cause ministers to enter and remain in the ministry would be helpful.

What are the motives of the ministers of this age? Let us name and examine some of them which are often expressed or vividly demonstrated.

One motive is that of *self-preservation,* or success without work. A man may enter the ministry and remain in its service simply as a result of merely personal consideration, that is, because he prefers it to any other of the leading professions or because he thinks it is an honorable way to earn a living or to spend one's life.

One's choice of the ministry may be based wholly on his lazy conception that it will not require as much work as other fields of endeavor. Such a man enters the ministry for the same reason that Amos and Andy's friend, the Kingfish, attempts a "new deal," namely, because he wants to avoid the gruesome reality of work. Concerning this class of ministers, I have but a brief prayer, "God save us from such ministerial leeches as soon as possible." Of all types of service in the world the ministry is the last in which a lazy man ought to be engaged.

But what of the man who is motivated by the noble desire to make a living for himself and perhaps a family? A Scottish parson was called from a poor to a wealthy church. Consulting with his beadle as to what to do, that wise functionary said, "Go where there is the most sin." Reflecting for a moment, he answered, "Then I ought to go where there is the most money." Such seems to be the reasoning of many ministers of this enlightened day. Is there any reason why one should not enter the ministry, as he would enter the mercantile or insurance business, for a living? Yes, a thousand times, yes. The ministry is not a business. Christ never brought His Church into existence to provide jobs for people. As world-girdling as is the Kingdom program, there is not one square inch in it for a job-seeker. Those who are thus motivated should read again the words of Ezekiel, "Woe be to the shepherds of Israel that do feed themselves." *

Surely, on this motive of self-preservation, with its attendant evils of pulpit-seeking by every means, of pulpit competition, at times even of salary undercutting and of common "chiseling" to get "bigger" pulpits, must fall the thunderous anathema of the ages. It has no more justification than has paganism to be mixed with Christianity. The Kingdom will suffer whenever and wherever it is burdened with ministerial job-holders. It is a cause for thanksgiving that there are not many preachers of this kind.

* Ezekiel 34:2.

A kindred motive to that of self-preservation, and, if anything, a far more reprehensible one, is that of *self-aggrandizement*. Some men apparently enter the ministry because it offers a desirable social distinction, or because it is "a business that offers pleasantly favorable chances for cultural leisure," coveted leadership or attractive publicity. Many in this class suffer from a disease called megalomania, which, being translated, is fame-o-mania. Some of them will stoop to any form of sensationalism, clownishness, or circus acts to get a crowd and coveted popularity. Others—"Oh, tell it not in Gath"—will use any means to get great numbers and occasionally even pad the roll to make favorable public impressions.

Some men keep the wires hot and the printer's devil on the run with self-publicity. These evidently try to fulfill the injunction contained in the text quoted by a Negro preacher, "Verily, verily, I says unto you, let every man blow his own trumpet, or it shall not be blowed." Others court "the powers that be" and use every political gymnastic imaginable to get that big city church or that coveted denominational office. And then there are the plagiarists who, too lazy to work themselves and yet desirous of being known as "great preachers," find it rather convenient to use the sermons of others! These all form a class of sometimes well-known and often influential individuals who, like the poor, "are always with us," but one wonders what will be their amazement and disappointment in that day when "the fire shall try every man's work of what sort it is." The motive of self-aggrandizement must be rejected as wholly unworthy.

A third motive, which I am made to believe is one of the chiefest in the number of its representatives in the ministry, is that of a *compelling sense of altruism*. What a noble motive this is! Who is not touched with compassion at the sight of real need? This fact is undoubtedly true of every real Christian.

After Emmet Stephens, a Georgia Baptist missionary who gave his life for Christ in China, had concluded his message one day, an aged Chinese gentleman tottered up to him and with a pathetic appeal in his voice said, "Sir, you came almost too late!" What soul is not moved by such an appeal? It must have been a similar appeal of the lame man at the gate of the temple called Beautiful which caused Peter to say, "Silver and gold have I none; but such as I have give I thee: in the name of Jesus Christ of Nazareth rise up and walk."

As noble, however, as is this motive, we search the New Testament in vain for the statement of any apostle that he was serving his Lord for this cause. Unquestionably, the apostles looked on the cases of need for their service and message with compassion like that of their Master, but this was not their chief cause for service. There is always a deeper motive evident for their self-denying, sacrificial labors.

The sense of altruism is an inadequate motive. It is based on our feelings and is without an imperatively needed higher authority for our services. It is freely granted that this would be a different place if every man in it were possessed of a sense of altruism. Christianity, in fact, demands altruism on the part of its professors. "As ye would that men should do unto you, do ye even so to them" is the loftiest and noblest standard for social behavior ever given to man. It demands the highest altruism. But this is not to say that altruism is the highest motive for service. The fact is that it needs a deeper motive back of it to make it abiding. Missionaries who have been known to go out to their fields wholly under the impulse of altruism also have been known soon to return. This motive by itself will not endure the strain.

A fourth motive for special Christian service is suggested by the text, *"It is more blessed to give than to receive."* But I cannot think that Jesus intended that this should be our chief motive for service, for the reason that, basically, it is a motive of acquisitiveness. It takes for granted our selfish desire to receive the most possible for ourselves and says frankly, "If you would get the largest return to yourself, do not try to be a receiver but be a giver. The giver makes the most in the long run. If you want to make an investment from which you will get the greatest return, then make it in giving."

Surely we must agree that the highest motive for the minister must be one in which there is no element of selfishness. On this basis the motive expressed in Christ's teaching, "It is more blessed to give than to receive," must be rejected as inadequate to be the supreme urge for our ministry.

We come now to the consideration of a fifth motive, namely, the *motive of inner compulsion.*

This is a motive which in some quarters has been relegated to archaism. One writer of a book on making ministers put the case as follows:

> The lure of the ministry as the most interesting, the most human, the most rewarding of all the callings open to the sons of men is casting its spell upon hundreds of young men of first-rate ability with real capacity for leadership. The number of long-faced theologues entering our divinity schools at this time and calling out sadly to their fellows, "Woe is me if I preach not the gospel," is happily very small. For that fact let us thank God and take courage! *

This writer seems jubilant that the "woe" has been lost from the countenance and conversation of our young theologues. We are to thank God and take courage—a big slice of courage—that the chair of "woe" has been removed from our seminaries as antique furniture.

But wait! It seems I have heard somewhere that antique furniture may sometimes be worth more than the new. Let us therefore be wise enough at least to investigate a moment before we discard it. We turn a moment to the Sole-Basis-For-Our-Authority-And-Practice. "But Peter and John answered and said unto them, Whether it be right in the sight of God to hearken unto you more than

---

* Charles R. Brown, *The Making of a Minister* Century Company, p. 8. 1927.

unto God, judge ye. For we cannot but speak the things
which we have seen and heard." * Again, "Woe is unto
me if I preach not the gospel." ** Or again, in the words
of a representative prophet, "Moreover, the word of the
Lord came to me, saying, Go and cry!" ***

If I know the Bible, the prophets of the Book served
under compulsion. God laid His hand on them and
they spoke "for holy men of God spake as they were
moved . . ." †

What I am saying is this: the prophets of old were men
"called" and men who *knew* they were called and men
who spoke and labored because they knew they were
called. They were men under divine compulsion. I ask,
when did this cease to be necessary? Is it a fact that we
have advanced so far ahead of God in these modern days
that we do not any longer need men who can stand before the throngs "where cross the crowded ways" and declare, "The word of the Lord came unto me, saying . . ."?

Yes, in spite of all our assumed modernity, we still need
God-called men who can face the multitudes and say with
profound sincerity, "Hear, hear the word of the Lord.
God has sent me with this message unto you."

Jesus was always under the divine imperative. "Know
ye not that I *must* be about my Father's business?" ††
Or, again, "I *must* work the works of him that sent me

* Acts 4:19, 20.
** I Cor. 9:16.
*** Jer. 2:1, 2.
† II Peter 1:21.
†† Luke 2:49.

while it is day." * If we would be like our Master, we shall be ministers under divine compulsion. Then we cannot help but say, "Woe is unto me if I preach not the gospel."

Give us men who are moved by the conviction that they are "called of God" to deliver a message from God and, though heaven and earth pass away, will be heard and their ministry be felt. Woe is unto the ministry in whose commission there is no "Must!"

But this is not the highest motive the Scriptures reveal for service. It is pure. It is abiding until one's work is done. But it is not adequate. Jonah had the call and was given the message, but it was not a motive sufficiently strong to keep him from running away. It is possible that some "Jonahs" may still be running from service.

Not very long ago the writer heard a Bible expositor, whose opinion he respects possibly more than that of any other man living, say that the motive for being "laborers together with God" ought to be the same as the motive which moves God. He went on to say that God is motivated by His own nature, by His own holiness and righteousness. He then declared that we ought to be similarly motivated, *that our nature within should become so pure and righteous that we would be caused to serve by what we have become within.*

In one breath I am almost ready to accept the expositor's conclusion. In another I hesitate. Somehow, I feel that it is too ideal. I hear Paul, whose holiness and right-

* John 9:4 (R.V.).

eousness overtower mine as the Alpine heights overtower an ant-hill, saying, "I am the chief of sinners. . . ." * "When I would do good evil is present. . . . What I would not, that I do. . . . O wretched man that I am, who shall deliver me from this vile body?" **

These statements do not excuse one for his shortcomings, but do give weight to the opinion that the motive designated by the Bible expositor is perhaps unattainable, except in a relative degree, this side of heaven.

Oh that we could attain unto it!

But if it is attainable, what shall be our motive for attempting to attain to this ideal estate? What would be the substitute or temporary motive that would serve adequately to enable us to reach the level of this ideal motive?

A final motive now presents itself for consideration. It was the declared motive of Paul and apparently the basic motive of every other New Testament servant of Christ. Let Paul give it in his own words, *"For the love of Christ constraineth us;* because we thus judge, that if one died for all, then were all dead: and that he died for all, that they which live should not henceforth live unto themselves, but unto him which died for them, and rose again." †

Paul is saying it is not primarily his love for Christ, but Christ's love for him that motivates him. What is more, Paul is specific about the manifestations of this love which

* I Tim. 1:15.
** See Romans 7:15-25.
† II Cor. 5:14-15.

have made it become the chief dynamic in his life. It was not primarily the manifestation of it in Christ's teaching ministry or the demonstration of it in His healing ministry which had the deepest influence over Paul. It was the love of Christ as revealed in His death and victory over sin and the grave that moved Paul. Like John, he would say, "Herein is love, not that we loved God, but that he loved us, and sent his Son to be the propitiation for our sins." * Paul could never get away from the Cross. He never cared to. For him Christianity was polarized at the Cross. The center of his universe and the supreme object of his glorying was the Cross of Jesus Christ. He determined to know nothing else among men save Jesus Christ and Him crucified. The reason is not difficult to see. Paul had found himself a sinner, the chief of sinners, dead in trespasses and in sins. Then he realized that Christ loved him enough to die for him that he might live. This fact became the supreme dynamic in his life. It was the love of Christ, the love made real to him in Christ's death for him, that became the indestructible motive for his indefatigable service. He would readily say with Isaac Watts:

> Love so amazing, so divine,
> Demands my soul, my life, my all.

What shall we say regarding motivation by Christ's constraining love? First of all, it must be granted that the motive is pure, is undefiled by any base element like

* I John 4:10.

selfishness. In the second place, the motive of Christ's constraining love is adequate. It has in it the power to eliminate base and unworthy practices. How can anyone motivated by Christ's love stoop to cheap pettifoggery in any phase of his Master's work? It is, in fact, the highest and mightiest motive for righteous living. When one is truly moved to service by Christ's Calvary-revealed love, he cannot bend to the level of the conduct of the world.

Christ's love is adequate in its urge to service. This love incomparable constrains men, first of all, to give *in* to Christ. No longer can one who has come to know His love hold out against Him. To experience its vitalizing and recreating power is to capitulate to it.

As His love constrains one to give *in* to Him; it likewise constrains one to give *over* to Him every power and faculty which one possesses.

> Such love constrains me to answer His call,
> Follow His leading and give Him my *all*.

The love of Christ also constrains one to give *out* for Him—to give out in word and in deed, to give out one's best and one's all. It causes one to give out for Him when the heavens are blue and the sun is shining benignly upon him; it *keeps* one giving out when the skies turn black and storms begin to break about him. It places a message upon one's lips and a song in one's heart when all goes pleasantly and every man seems ready to hear and to heed; it *keeps* the same message on his lips and even adds courage to the song in his heart when disappointment seems to be the only reward and when no man seems willing to hear or to heed. Regardless of the changing of tide and time, it prompts perennial faithfulness. It makes one invulnerable until his work is done.

Yes, the incomparable love of the peerless Christ constitutes a pure, adequate, and an abiding motive. The George Mathesons of the ministry may for the moment find their devotion divided on some inferior object of affection, but when the swelling current of His heaven-born love flows in, they will always rise to say:

> O Love that wilt not let me go,
> I rest my weary soul in Thee;
> I give Thee back the life I owe,
> That in Thine ocean depths its flow
> May richer, fuller be!

4. The Minister and His Conduct

A business man holding a ranking executive position in an important concern of one of our great cities invited the writer to lunch with him one day in order that he might discuss with him some personal problems relating to his spiritual life. This man, the father of two most promising medical doctors, came, as a patient to his doctor, for advice. In the course of the conversation mention was made of a former pastor of the business man. The latter then remarked, "I could never go to him for spiritual advice. I never felt that I cared to open my heart to him. You see, Mr. *Blank* is a *clown*."

"My pastor is a clown." What a characterization for a minister of Jesus Christ!

No, the business man in question is not a dyspeptic sort of person. Far from it. He is an affable fellow who really enjoys fun. He told, as a matter of fact, how he had enjoyed having the preacher referred to in his home on numerous occasions, and how this preacher had always kept things lively with his antics, but—and this is the significant point—he did not "care" to discuss the deep matters of his spiritual life with this man. The business man looked on the preacher as merely a clever clown!

No doubt this preacher thought himself popular with

the business man. He was well received. His antics were evidently enjoyed. But what a tragedy! If he had only known it, he had chosen to be a court fool rather than to be his Lord's ambassador.

The pastor under discussion was quite a popular fellow. He was usually the center of a group watching his antics or listening to his witticisms with avidity. Perhaps he is envied by many of his less popular and entertaining fellow ministers. But the title given him by the business man who, as a matter of information, was one of this preacher's former deacons (and a loyal one at that) is not enviable. For a minister of Jesus Christ and a herald of the Gospel to be called a clown is not complimentary. Much less complimentary is it for a minister to conduct himself in such a way that his people do not care to consult him in spiritual matters and will not open their hearts to him.

Ministers, it is freely admitted, ought to be pleasant and winsome, and, at times, even entertaining, but no minister can afford to become a clown. With what dignity, with what grace, with what consciousness of the loftiness of his office ought an ambassador of the King of kings carry himself.

The world at such a time as this, or at any time, will never be saved by ministers who are court fools instead of Christ's true ambassadors. The admonition of Paul, "Let no man despise thee," does not mean that one should endeavor to be popular, but, on the contrary, that one should so live as to avoid the contempt of men. It is discouraging, if not heart-rending, to see how often men seek popularity. Sometimes they appear to be willing to have it at any price. They adopt tricks of showmanship and even clownish rôles to gather a crowd. All the while they forget that they have chosen the part of a court fool. As a consequence, the Gospel and the ministry are cheapened immeasurably.

Dr. George W. Truett used to say, "Terrible is it beyond all words for Christ's preacher to be the wrong kind of a man. The Christian ministry is not for prigs and fops and charlatans." *

Of course, it must not be assumed that there is any great number of "prigs and fops and charlatans" in the ministry. The requirements of the ministry are such as to eliminate most of this kind before they are hardly begun. But the fact remains that it is possible for any minister to bring contempt on the cause he represents by careless behavior. One can become a court fool without realizing it, probably without even wanting to do it.

The writer knows a minister who preached a whole sermon on his knees and one who preached in overalls. It was not the intention in either case, apparently, to become sensational, but both methods of delivering the sermon proved ill-chosen. People misinterpreted the motive. The message was cheapened in the eyes of many of those present in each case.

Years ago another preacher of some fame conducted a

* *Follow Thou Me,* Sunday School Board of the Southern Baptist Convention, 1932, 232.

service in a church. He came not by the choice of the
pastor but by the request of certain members of the
church. His service lasted for about two hours, most of
which time was spent in "wise-cracking" and in other
vain endeavors to entertain his audience. Only fifteen
minutes of his time was consumed by his message.
One prominent leader in the church, chairman then of
the school board in that large community, became so in-
dignant over the program of this minister that he walked
out of the service before it was half over. Many others
of the church characterized the performance as a "cheap
vaudeville" or "a minstrel show." It required months to
heal the hurt done to the church in that one service. Yet
it is doubtless a fact that this particular preacher constantly conducts services similar to the one put on in that
church. Although he wins a following and it cannot be
proved that he does not do some good, it may be properly
questioned whether his method does not seriously cheapen
his message and the work of the ministry among a large
number of people. It is a fact that many lay Christians
look on him as a court fool.

But the worst danger and one which should give every
minister concern is that of weakening his ministry and
hurting his influence by his daily conduct. The tragedy
of tragedies for the Christian minister is to make people
feel that he is too frivolous and light-hearted or too lacking in spiritual depth and concern for them to want to
open their hearts to him. Such was the case of the minister referred to in the opening of this chapter. Yet there

are ministers who will tell "shady" and even vulgar stories and some who swear and use border-line profanity. There are others who carry joking and pranks to an extreme.

A friend of the writer told him of how a church of which he was pastor was almost wrecked by the pranks and careless talk, sometimes bordering on the "shady" side, of his predecessor in his relationships with the young people of the church. More than once the writer has heard of ministers whom the men of the church did not want to visit their wives when they were not present. Such a condition is little short of calamitous. Especially is this true when by some unintentional act or careless story one has raised suspicions, while in his heart he may be as trustworthy as an angel. The integrity of a minister ought to be so guarded in every act and word that men may trust him anywhere and under all circumstances.

One of the most essential duties of the minister is to be a spiritual adviser. He should covet and do all in his power to cultivate the confidence of his people to the degree that they will be willing and will feel free to open their hearts to him. In this way he will be able to do some of his mightiest work.

Who could imagine Peter or James or John or Paul telling, or even listening to, a "smutty" story or engaging in a clownish act? Although they were not always above reproach, yet they counted it a privilege to be ambassadors of their Lord and endeavored to conduct themselves accordingly. Elisha was, doubtless, pleasant "company" in the Shunamnite's home, but he so conducted himself that his hostess saw in him a man of such godliness and integrity that she felt free to unburden the deep things of her soul to him. How precious he became to that home. But he meant no more to that home than any minister may mean to any number of homes in this day. Concerning everything that would hinder a minister from having this high privilege, the charge of Paul becomes pertinent, "But thou, O man of God, flee these things." *

Woodrow Wilson spoke words which deserve the heed of every living preacher when he said:

> The world is not going to be evangelized; the church is not going to uncover its authority among men until its ministers display their credentials in their lives by showing that the thought that is in them is always the thought that makes for salvation; that they will not teach the things that are impure; that they will not play the things that are dangerous.
>
> You do not have to be anything in particular to be a lawyer. You do not have to be anything apart, except a kindhearted man, to be a physician. . . . The *only* profession which consists in being something is the ministry of our Lord and Saviour—*and it does not consist of anything else.*** And that conception of the minister which rubs all marks of it off and mixes him in the crowd so that you cannot point him out, is a process of eliminating the ministry itself.†

* I Tim. 6:11.
** Of course, it does consist in some other things besides "being something," as elsewhere set forth in these pages.
† Quoted in *The Layman Measures The Minister,* Leavell, Sunday School Board, 1930, p. 24.

Pity of pities it is if a minister through careless talk, or even listening to such, or through unguarded acts, gives the impression that he is not a good ambassador of Christ. It is said of Robert E. Lee that he never told a story that would not have been acceptable in mixed company, nor would he listen to such. When someone in the act of telling a story, began with the remark, "Are there any women present?" Lee replied, "No, but there are gentlemen present." The story was not told. No minister should be less a gentleman than was General Lee.

The warning of this chapter must not be taken as an objection to humor on the part of the minister. The fact is that humor is "the saving sense," even with the minister. Blessed is that minister who has a native sense of humor. The others ought to cultivate it! But one's humor should be of right proportion and of high character. It should not be overdone, so that one will be taken as light-hearted, nor should wit ever be debased to the suggestive.

"You must come up to a much higher level than common manhood if you mean to be a preacher," were the warning words of one of America's greatest ministers.*

With the preacher it is even more true than with others that what he does—and says—speaks so loudly, if it is bad, that one cannot hear what he says. Truly, "manhood is the best sermon." Let every minister then take heed that he be a real man and true gentleman that men may see in him always a genuine ambassador of the Most High. "If a preacher is a true man," said Beecher, "(and

*Henry Ward Beecher, in Yale *Lectures On Preaching,* p. 37.

a true man spreads out and covers with himself all times and all places) he preaches not only while he is in the pulpit; but just as much when he is conversing with a little child on the sidewalk, when he is in a social company, or when he is on a sportive or picnic occasion with his people."

It is comparatively easy to be a court fool, but it takes the highest type of discipline to become a true ambassador of Christ. Let every minister remember, however, that, not by means of court fools, but through His chosen servants who pay the price of real ambassadorship will God be able to give leadership to the salvaging of this sinking, sin-sick, suicidal world.

The true minister will say with the earnestness of an affirmation of faith, "I am not here to play, to entertain or to be cheaply popular," but

"Ambassador to be of realms beyond the sea,
I'm here on business for my King." *

* Hope Publishing Co. (c)

5. THE MINISTER AND HIS METHOD

There are two distinct classes of ministers that are direct opposites. There is the lion type of minister and there is the lamb type. The lion type is strong-willed, forceful, and courageous. He spends most of his time fighting something. The lamb type is modest, gentle, inoffensive, and cautious. He rarely gets into a fight. He never provokes serious opposition. He prefers serenity, though frequently he is not allowed to enjoy it. In times such as these it is important that these two types be examined carefully, that they may be known and avoided.

Of the two types which one may be said to be preferable? Neither. Both miss the mark for the minister. Both create serious problems. The cause of Christ is frequently hurt by a pugnacious preacher. Churches are often split by them. Sinners are offended by them. The world cannot harmonize their temperament with that of the lowly Nazarene. They seem too unlike their Master.

The lamb-like minister also creates problems. Because he is afraid of giving offense, evil may go on untouched or even uncondemned. This may lead to serious difficulties in the church. It will cause the church to be too tolerant of the sins of its community. The work of such a minister is likely to be nonaggressive and, consequently, the church goes backward, and at times very nearly dies. It ceases to have the respect of the community or the favor of God.

I

What is the trouble with the lamb-like preacher? It is mainly that there are some needed qualities lacking. Certainly some of the attributes of the lamb-like preacher are desirable. He is to be commended, for instance, for his humility and meekness of spirit, but, in addition to these virtues, he must have others which are almost, if not fully, as important.

The lamb-like preacher needs *courage*. One must be able to face the rich without timidity, the political official without reticence, and the brutal or the bully, without fear. He must have that inner fortitude which will enable him to make clear the will of God, to condemn wrong and to call to service without flinching. This is his mission as an ambassador of Christ. Genuine courage and Christlike humility do not mutually exclude each other, as some men seem to think; but they may be coexistent. As was John the Baptist, who was so humble that he felt himself unworthy to loose the latchet on the shoes of the Master, and yet was so brave that he could face a murderous Herod with condemnation for the latter's guilt in marrying his brother's wife, so must the true minister be. The rank, power, and brutality of Herod were not able to shake the courage of John. So it must be with every truly successful minister who is faithful to his responsibility.

The lamb-like minister needs also the virtue of *aggressiveness*. Characteristically, the lamb-like preacher is easy-going and nonprogressive. Because of caution about offending people and his fear of taking a strong stand on any issue, he allows things to drift along the easiest course. Few, if any, churches will grow under such leadership. No church will drift into success. The nonaggressive minister has marked off for himself a stand-still, if not a retrogressive, ministry.

The lamb-like minister, furthermore, needs a *steel will against evil and compromise*. The greatest peril to the gentle, timid type of preacher probably lies just here. He is easily "run over" or forced into compromising positions. For the minister of Christ this is tragic. He can never afford to compromise on a principle or to give in on a moral issue. The moment he does so, he immediately forfeits his rights to Christian leadership. Of course, there is hardly a day in the carrying on of the minister's work when one is not confronted with some matter the easiest way to deal with which would be to wink at the evil involved or to compromise a shade in relationship to it. We do well to pray that God make the preachers strong and true in every such hour of temptation and trial. But how often the lamb-like preacher fails under such circumstances!

A fourth quality definitely needed by the lamb-like

preacher is *strength in his personality which will inspire confidence in himself as a leader.* A shrinking personality never inspires confidence. One who is reticent and timid is a failure as a leader. A dynamic, strong personality is required to make one able to inspire others to follow him. But what is a minister who cannot lead? He is about as valuable as a surgeon without arms, a watch-repairman without hands or a soldier without sight. The minister's work depends daily on leadership. He cannot drive, nor demand, nor compel. *All he can legitimately do is to lead.* The people can heed or ignore him if they choose. Other than the authority which comes from his claim of having been sent of God, he has no actual power to demand anything of the people. He must persuade. "We persuade men," * wrote Paul, and we may be sure he knew what he was saying. How else shall one persuade men if his personality is weak? If one fails to be able to persuade men, what can be the hope of his ministry?

II

But if the lamb-like preacher is undesirable, so also is the lion-like preacher, though for quite another reason. While the former fails because of timidity, fear, hesitancy and the lack of positiveness, the latter comes short mainly because of overworking certain qualities which might be virtues on a milder scale. The lion type of minister is courageous, aggressive, steel-willed, one who will not com-

* II Cor. 5:11.

promise. He is usually a man of strong personality who can evoke great confidence in and loyalty to his leadership on the part of those who see his way. But here is the pity of it, there are not usually many who can be made to see his way. Too often he repels when he needs to win. He creates strong resentments and antagonisms. He has enemies and creates enmities. Meetings are frequently made stormy occasions by his type, and churches are often broken asunder. The peace of Christ hardly has a chance to rule the hearts of the people where he has a part. The wreckage sometimes caused by him is tragic, and in some cases it requires generations to remove it.

What is the trouble with the lion-like preacher? The answer is not difficult. First, *it is hard for him to see the viewpoint of others.* He knows he is right and resents a contrary attitude. He is resolved, moreover, to force others to see his way. Although one may be commended for having strong opinions and for supporting those opinions, nevertheless, it is a pitiful thing for one not to be able to see the point of view of others. For one reason, it is possible for anybody to be wrong sometimes, even a preacher! But the main reason for the tragedy of such a condition as is being described is that a minister, though he be absolutely right in his own stand, needs to understand and be sympathetic with the attitude of others, in order that he may best be able to lead them to the right position. How important this fact is in getting over one's own convictions!

Another trouble with the lion-like preacher is *that he is too uncompromising.* Such is possible. Of course, one should never compromise in a matter which involves a principle, but there are many things which do not involve principles and on which a minister can well afford to be agreeable. Take, for instance, methods of procedure, organizational setup, or other matters of routine as examples. One ought to seek to be agreeable in these things. Often a compromise between the plan of the pastor and the desire of the people may prove best in the long run. Sometimes the adoption of a compromise plan may be the speediest way to reach the ideal. It may serve as a temporary expedient until the people can be better prepared for the preferred plan. The point is, any minister can well afford to practice moderation and conciliation in matters which do not demand a moral or theological compromise which would violate one's conscience. There are many churches which could have been saved from serious splits if only their pastors had seen the wisdom of following this course. But the lion-like preacher will refuse to do it. He is willing to sacrifice peace and harmony to carry his point.

A third difficulty with the lion-like type of minister is *that he usually repels those who do not agree with* him. His belligerent way forces antagonism to rise. He makes those who do not fall in line with him his opponents. This is unfortunate for a minister. He ought to covet the ability to remain firm in his stand for right and at the same time keep the esteem and even the love of those with whom he must disagree. This is the only way he will ever win over those who are in the wrong. He cannot win them when he allows them to become his opponents or when he repels them by belligerency.

Probably the worst fault the lion-like preacher has, however, *is his tendency to become a dictator.* He is domineering and demanding. He must have his way. He will brook no opposition to his program. Consequently, for the sake of harmony, the people allow him to take the rôle of a dictator. How unfortunate this usually proves to be! People will not endure a dictator indefinitely. In time they will be provoked to arise in opposition. Then division is bound to come and great hurt may ensue. At best, the church which is run very long by a man of this type will, when he is gone, be likely to flounder. It will not know how to run itself with its "head" gone. More than one church of this kind has come upon sad days. The writer knows an outstanding case of a church that was in charge of a certain minister for some forty-five years. After the minister's death, the church was lost, not knowing what to do or how to carry on its work. Evil days followed. Of course, this case was exceptional. Ordinarily the church will not submit to the dictator very long, but rises in opposition. Then disturbances come which may cost many souls and well nigh wreck the church.

Ministers are not called to be dictators, but shepherds. As shepherds they should lovingly lead the flock, not drive it. A driven flock will be a divided flock before long.

What, then, is needed in the minister is that he shall be neither a lion nor a lamb. The ideal is a well-balanced, finely-blended combination of the best qualities of both types. Such is the minister Paul describes:

> ... *Giving no offence in any thing, that the ministry be not blamed:* but in all things approving ourselves as the ministers of God, in much patience, in afflictions, in necessities, in distresses, in stripes, in imprisonments, in tumults, in labours, in watchings, in fastings; by pureness, by knowledge, by longsuffering, by kindness, by the Holy Ghost, by love unfeigned, by the word of truth, by the power of God, by the armour of righteousness on the right hand and on the left, by honour and dishonour, by evil report and good report: as deceivers, and yet true; as unknown, and yet well known; as dying, and behold, we live; as chastened and not killed; as sorrowful, yet alway rejoicing; as poor, yet making many rich; as having nothing, and yet possessing all things.*

* II Cor. 6:3-10.

6. THE MINISTER AND HIS MASTER KEY

What is the master key to the hearts of the people and to success in the work of the ministry? This, one who is awake to the needs of these times, will want to know. Is it education? Is it specialized training in the methods of running a church? Is it personality? Is it sermonic and oratorical ability? Is it consecration and fidelity, or what is it?

Education of the highest order is greatly needed, if, indeed, circumstances do not require it, of the minister in this day. But education is by no means the minister's mightiest instrument. Almost anyone can name men of brilliance intellectually and of high educational attainments who are practically failures in the pulpit. They may make a success at teaching, but churches die under them. So true is this that some people have concluded that to be intellectual and well trained educationally cuts one off from the people, that one of such attainment is almost necessarily cold and aloof and consequently a poor pastor. Such need not be the case, however, as can be demonstrated in numerous instances. The trouble is, some men overlook the fact that a good education is not in itself a guarantee of success. Although it should be an advantage to anyone, if depended upon solely it may allow one to be a grand "flop" instead of aiding him to be a great success. It is assuredly not the minister's master key.

Specialized training in the mechanics and methods of running a church does not necessarily guarantee success. Although it will prove a great asset to any minister, it is not his master key. The writer has observed more than one minister who was most efficient at organization and who had mastered the art of conducting a worship service, whose church nevertheless slowly shriveled under him.

A fine personality is one of the most valuable assets any person may possess, but for the minister it becomes almost imperative. Without a good personality there are already nine counts against any minister even before he begins. This fact makes it urgent, indeed, that one give constant heed to the development of his personality, taking every advantage of every means of help that may come within his grasp. But, after all this is said, it must be added that not even a good personality is the master key to the hearts of men. A few men with outstanding personalities have been known to be colossal failures. Some, on the other hand, with poor personalities, have been able to do an abiding work. It may be doubted, in view of some of the allusions in his letters to criticisms which had been made against him, that Paul himself had a very winsome or impressive personality. Yet Paul had a master key to the hearts of men, and few, if any, have equaled his success.

Sermonic and oratorical ability are to be coveted by every preacher of the Gospel. How we ought to strive to attain to higher and higher levels in these requirements!

But more than once has it been said to the writer, "Dr. Blank is a masterful preacher, but he is a failure as a pastor. Although his sermons are great discourses and are delivered in a superb manner, still he fails to get the hearts of the people." Evidently in such a case some essential element is missing. Great preaching ability is crucially needed, but it is not the minister's most certain avenue to success.

Surely consecration and fidelity are essential for any lasting success in the ministry, but, strangely enough, alone, they do not bring success. It has often been wondered by many people why certain men, fully consecrated and notedly faithful, seemed never to be able to make the grade. Of course, various factors may be the cause of failure, such as personality limitations, eccentricities or hobby riding; but there is one element which, if added to the virtues of consecration and fidelity, will almost invariably guarantee success.

What is that quality which is most basic to ministerial success? The answer is clear. *It is a burning, compassionate, heaven-born love for the people.* This is the minister's most effective instrument. This is his *master key.*

Love makes preaching more effective. At least, it makes it more effective than it would be otherwise. Dr. James A. Maxwell, successful pastor for many years and for nearly two decades a dearly beloved seminary professor, has often been heard by the writer to say, "Young men, love the flock. If you love them, you can preach anything and they will think it is good. You can say your multiplication table backwards and they will go away, saying, 'My, wasn't that a great sermon!'" Of course, this was an obvious exaggeration to emphasize a point, but there is enough truth in it to merit consideration. Correction and even condemnation will be accepted without resentment by the people when they know that it comes from a heart that loves them.

Someone has told of having heard a family speak in the most glowing terms of what a great preacher they had at their church. Then he had opportunity to hear the preacher himself. Being disappointed at the ordinary sermon he heard, he mentioned it to the family. They replied, "Oh, but he *is* a great preacher. You see, he loves the people so." That is the answer. Ordinary preaching may be great preaching to the people if it arises out of a heart that is a fountain of love. After all, great preaching cannot be measured by any standard yardstick. It must be measured by how effectively it plays on the chords of men's souls.

Love wins the people. There are few people who cannot be won by love. They may be cold and aloof at first, but love can burn the barriers down. One of the writer's most intimate friends was a deacon in a church the writer formerly served as pastor. At the time when he went to this church this deacon simply froze him with his aloofness and coldness. The deacon had some suspicions about the theology and methods of his new pastor, and, consequently, although he had not opposed the call, he had apparently resolved to be wholly unco-operative. But gradually the process of love worked. Before the end of the pastorate, the deacon had become the preacher's warmest and most valued friend in the church. The affection between them now is as fine as that of brothers. This was no ordinary case. Neither arguments nor any other means than love could have brought about such a radical change.

Love binds the people. The most effective way—in fact, the only way—to bind a people to one's self as a pastor is to love the people. The bonds which love can build are stronger than bands of steel. They will hold when all else fails. How full of meaning are the words of the writer of Proverbs, "Love is strong as death." A certain minister went to a church which was split four ways. One cause of the division in the church was over theology, which is one of the most serious problems of all to solve. The pastor decided, however, to love the people. He loved one theological faction as well as another, although at no time compromising his own message. He loved one group of those who held personal animosities toward another group as well as he loved the other group. Soon love worked and every barrier was burned away and the people were melted into one body whose unity of fellowship seemed like that of a large family. The preacher used as a text for an anniversary sermon at the close of his third year as pastor there Paul's declaration to the church at Philippi, "I have you in my heart." * That, in so far as the human element was concerned, was the secret of the new unity of the people. Because the pastor had them "in his heart,"

* Phil. 1:7.

he had not only bound them to himself but had been the cause of their becoming bound to one another in brotherly love. Is not this the New Testament way?

Love moves the people. Beecher termed the "love-principle as the central power in the work of a Christian minister." He further remarked, "There is only one pass-key that will open every door, and that is the golden key of love. You can touch every side of the human heart and its every want, that is, if you can touch it at all; and if you have the power to bestow anything, love gives facility of access, the power of drawing near unto men, the power of enriching thought, of weakening their hungry desires and appetites, the power to thaw out the winter of their souls and to prepare the soil for the seed and growth of the better life." * Beecher never spoke more profoundly and truthfully. When entreaty and argument and logic and condemnation all fail, love will succeed. These other elements are needed in a fruitful ministry, but they are well-nigh worthless unless they are mixed with genuine love.

Love opens the hearts of people. "No one can deal with the hearts of men as he ought, unless he has the sympathy which is given by love." How difficult it is to reach the hearts of some people; but few there are who are so petrified in heart that they are unmoved by the warmth and service of love. Frequently, even embittered and prejudiced souls have been won by ministers who have laid

* Yale *Lectures on Preaching,* Vol. I, p. 242.

siege to them with love-motivated acts of kindness and self-forgetful service. "Love never faileth."

Love calls forth the love of the people. When one hears a minister complain about not having the love of his people, one may, with fair safety, conclude that the pastor has not lost much love on the people. Love begets love. This is its nature. If one wants the love of his people, let him build the fire of love high in his own heart. There is no other way. "We love him because he first loved us."

Love reveals Christ in the minister's face. This is the highest service of love and the chief reason the minister should look to his own heart with diligent care. No matter what the minister does or what he may say or how he may do or say it, there is little possibility of any success without love. The reason is that where love is absent, Christ cannot be seen and if Christ be not seen in a minister his efforts are doomed. "If I can speak with the tongues of men and angels, but have not love, I am a blaring trumpet or a clanging cymbal. Or if I can prophesy and am versed in all mysteries and all knowledge, and have such absolute faith that I can remove mountains, but have not love, I am nothing. And if I use all I have to feed the poor, and give my body to be burned, but have not love, it profits me nothing." *

This gem of Pauline wisdom has its fullest meaning for preachers. Let them never fail to heed its warning.

In "The Deserted Village," Oliver Goldsmith has

* I Cor. 13:1-3, Weymouth.

painted the minister with the loving heart in these unforgettable words:

> A man he was to all the country dear . . .
> To them his heart, his love, his griefs, were given.

When such was the case, it is no wonder that:

> The service past, around the pious man,
> With ready zeal each honest rustic ran;
> E'en children follow'd, with endearing wile,
> And plucked his gown, to share the good man's smile.*

* "The Deserted Village," Columbia University Press.

7. THE MINISTER AND HIS HUMAN RELATIONS

Since the day Cain sought to excuse himself concerning the welfare of his brother whom he had slain, men have been considering the question, "Am I my brother's keeper?" Closely linked to this question have been other questions: To what extent am I my brother's keeper? What is the nature of my responsibility toward him? Under what circumstances and how long am I responsible?

These are such age-old questions that to many people they have become trite, but to the thoughtful student of life they are ever bristling with interest and importance, especially in these times. And of all men, to the wide-awake minister of the blessed Gospel they are most important. In fact, the minister's human relations are so vital that they are second in importance to, and only to, his personal relations to God through Christ.

If any man, and especially the minister, would learn the nature of his relation to his fellow man, let him learn from the Master of men. Jesus set forth in unmistakable terms in His teachings, such as that of the Good Samaritan,* the final judgment,** the Sermon on the Mount,***

* Luke 10:33.
** Matt. 25:31-46.
*** Matt. 5, 6, 7.

and numerous other expressions, how men should deal with their fellows. It is all summed up in one statement: namely, "Inasmuch as ye have done it unto one of the least of these my brethren, ye have done it unto me." * He thus revealed a matter of tremendous importance, which is the fact that in all our human relations we are not dealing merely man to man, but with Christ also.

The minister, then, in determining the nature and extent of his human relations must keep this declaration of Jesus in mind. In deciding what course he shall pursue to meet any human problem, his first question should be, "What is God's will concerning me, His minister and servant, in this matter?"

Certain general statements may be made, and with emphasis, concerning the minister and his human relations. First, he should recognize himself to be *a citizen* of the place in which he lives. He ought, in fact, to think of himself as a leader in the matter of citizenship. He is, or ought to be, an example in this as in other respects.

He should be a law-abiding citizen. The same inspired writer who declared that we who are in Christ are no longer under the law but under grace also declared, "Let every soul be subject unto the higher powers. For there is no power but of God: the powers that be are ordained of God. Whosoever therefore resisteth the power, resisteth the ordinance of God.** Sad it is indeed that even concerning some such common things as obeying traffic regu-

* Matt. 25:40.
** Rom. 13:1-2.

lations and speed laws some people feel that it is all right
if they can only "get by" with these infringements. The
same man who fails to include all of his earnings in his
income tax report, for example, because he thinks nobody
will ever know the difference, may later be overtempted
to take money from the church treasury when the church
officials are not watching. It should never be said of a
minister that he is a law-breaker. He may not favor certain laws, but his efforts to change them should not be in
the form of breaking or disregarding them, unless, of
course, they are laws which force him to do an immoral
thing or are an offense to his conscience. In such a case
he should prefer to die rather than to obey, even as did
many of our forefathers.

The minister should be a tax-payer. As a citizen his
responsibility in this matter is as great in proportion to
his possessions as is that of others. If possible, his tax
should be paid as soon as it is due. He should be sure that
he makes his tax returns properly.

He should be a voter. This is a most serious obligation.
He should never be a politician or partisan. He ought to
make it his duty to find out the principles involved and
the character of the office seekers. It is his duty to vote
according to his convictions. This means he should vote
as he prays. A further duty of the minister than merely
voting and knowing how he is voting, is to be a positive,
militant leader in moral reform. His unbounded duty,
enforced by the example of practically every Old Testament prophet and by Christ himself, is to denounce in

clear and forceful terms all moral evils and corruption. He should know that he is right and then be fearless in his leadership of the right. He may be denounced by the unscrupulous, but they will fear him and good men will admire him. A ministerial coward, afraid to utter his convictions on vital matters, is a reproach to the Lord and to His cause. When he remains unspotted in his character and rises above all efforts on the part of individuals, parties, or cliques to make of him a tool for their purposes, men will trust and admire him secretly if they do not openly. Though the minister does not—dare not—stoop to politics, let him do his utmost to lift it from "the gutter" and to abolish its corruptions.

The minister should be exceedingly *careful in money matters*. He should meet his financial obligations promptly if possible. If he cannot pay certain bills when they are due, he should make satisfactory arrangements concerning them before they fall due. In fact, the Scriptural injunction to "owe no man anything" is the best possible policy for the minister to follow. If he must borrow, it should be from those outside his community or place of labor, certainly not from his own flock. He should be business-like in all financial matters of the church. He should also insist on the church's being prompt and careful in all its business relations. Slipshod handling of personal business or other affairs for which he is responsible will not be tolerated on the part of any minister.

He should be a community builder. This does not mean that he is to become the leader necessarily or even a member of welfare or improvement committees, but that he shall give his co-operation in word and spirit to all such constructive efforts.

The matter of *law enforcement* is a ticklish problem. Shall the minister report all known offenders of the law, or is there a better way? If he takes another way, is he defeating the purposes of law and thereby failing to act the part of a good citizen? Certainly a good citizen should insist on staunch enforcement of the law, which demands that he shall not be a shield either willingly or through lack of concern to any offender. The minister must first remember, however, that his chief responsibility is a spiritual one. If he knows some young culprit or minor offender, or even one guilty of more serious offense, he should first go to that person as a Christian friend and do his utmost in the name and by the help of the Lord to lead him to the right. In many instances, the offender will not only be made to cease his offense and possibly be helped spiritually, but he will also be persuaded to make known his offense and to accept his just penalty. In most cases the punishment is suspended. If by this method the pastor can save a soul and a life, it is a blessed service, for "he that winneth souls is wise."

There will be certain cases, however, which it will be the minister's duty to report immediately. He should always be known, though, both as a friend to the enforcement of law and also as a friend to those in trouble and those who are "down and out." This is so important a fact that even the courts recognize the immunity of the minister from testifying concerning a confession made to him as a minister of God. Except in a case in which violent harm has been done to others by the confessor and the confessor refuses to surrender himself to the proper representatives of the law, it is entirely fitting that the minister take advantage of his immunity and keep all confessions not of the above character strictly confidential. Every effort ought to be made, however, to see that one who confesses a crime surrenders himself to the court.

A second question concerning the minister's human relations is, *What is his responsibility as a teacher?* It should be said, in the first place, that unless the sermon has in it, to a marked degree, the element of teaching, it falls far short of what it ought to be. The ministry by all means must be a teaching ministry if it is to be a building ministry. Closely related in the Gospel story are the statements that "Jesus came into Galilee, *preaching* the gospel of the kingdom of God" * and that "he *taught* them as one that had authority." **

The minister's life should teach. By his scholarly example, by his favorable attitude toward learning, and by his guidance of others, he will teach. People will follow him in this respect as in others.

It is wise that the minister know the fundamental principles of education. He should be familiar with educational psychology. He should equal, if not excel, in teaching ability any teacher who may sit in his congrega-

* Mark 1:14.
** Mark 1:22.

tion. His life is, or should be, a life of teaching as much so as the life of any instructor who ever entered a school-room.

The minister has a responsibility in relation to the school. He should be known as a friend to educational interests. He should seek to knit ties of friendship between himself and the schoolteachers, especially in towns, villages and small communities. To the best of his ability he should lead in co-operation between the church and school in the interest of the children. The ever-widening gulf between the church and school is creating a condition far from wholesome. It is the minister's duty to take the lead in an effort to bridge the gulf. Friendship that is not expressed in constructive, helpful service is worth little indeed.

One other place where the pastor's responsibility for teaching is great is the home. He should first attempt to make his own home a model. Then by sermon and by private conversation he should seek to lead parents into making homes in which Christ is given pre-eminence. To persuade a home to establish a family altar, for example, is an achievement great enough to make the angels in heaven rejoice.

Above all, he should remember that he is a teacher of things eternal, and that by example and by word he is teaching something either for good or for bad every day he lives.

Another question concerning the minister and his human relations is, *What are his duties as a neighbor?* On being a neighbor, in the popular sense of the term, a few things should be kept in mind. First, the minister should be an agreeable neighbor. It may be necessary at times for him to "turn the other cheek" in order to do it, but it will pay in the long run. He should see that the appearance of his home, in so far as he is able to govern it, is satisfactory. He should be careful that no conduct about the home may be cause of offense or of stumbling to his neighbors. He and his family should lend willingly, but never borrow if avoidable. The minister should practice friendliness with neighbors, and, if possible, should come to know them personally. There is danger in his overlooking the spiritual welfare of those about his own door.

In the story of the Good Samaritan, Jesus makes forever plain the answer to the question as to who is our neighbor. If the minister would be a real neighbor let him study how he may be a help to his needy fellow man. His should be a life of true neighborliness, of real helpfulness. He should know no class distinction. Neither poverty nor wealth, nor learning nor color should make any difference. The attitude in which he serves also is of tremendous importance. The lesson in Lowell's "Vision of Sir Launfal" can never be known too well. If his service or money be given in the spirit of the young searcher after the Holy Grail its value will be insignificant; but if it is given in the spirit of brotherly love its value is inestimable. Even a cup of cold water given in Jesus's name does not lose its reward.

Probably the most important of the minister's human

relations is the *minister as a friend.* It is in this sphere that the severest tests and obligations are brought to bear on him. Of all human relations outside of marriage, true friendship is the most valuable. Jesus suggested the value of it when He said, "Henceforth I call you not servants; for the servant knoweth not what his lord doeth; but I have called you friends; for all things that I have heard of my Father I have made known to you." * If Jesus designated the relation between Himself and His disciples as that of friendship, then friendship must be indeed a lofty and sacred relation.

By all means the minister should have close personal friends. He has a right to them, and he will certainly need them. They are not to take the place of Christ, the Friend of friends, but there will come times in the minister's life when his true friends will be worth more than all the world to him. When in his desperate fight for the right there come times during which it seems that all the world has either misunderstood, or else has become an enemy to him, he will learn to prize his friends most highly.

Not only will true friends be of value in times of trouble, but they will at all times be a blessing. Their advice and their constructive criticism are inestimable. "Faithful are the wounds of a friend."

Since there is so much at stake, the minister should be very careful in selecting personal friends. They should be of the finest type, people of character and culture. Their financial condition should be of no consequence, though

* John 15:15.

friendship with wealthy people should not be avoided merely because the people are wealthy. In every case they should be of the type that will be an uplift, at least in some particular way. Some may be a benediction spiritually, others intellectually. Some may broaden one's knowledge by their experience in travel, others by their literary culture. Some by their legal, sociological or political relations may give one a better insight into the condition of the cold, grim world of the masses; others may fructify the minister's mind and add meat to his message by their knowledge of art, botany, biology, and the like. Friendships should be cultivated that are expanding to the soul and illuminating to the mind. "Iron sharpeneth iron; so a man sharpeneth the countenance of his friend."

Two cautions are in order. First, the minister should be careful in cultivating friendship not to lose sight of his major duties. It is very easy for one to allow the joy of communion with his friends to influence him into spending an unjustifiable amount of time in their company when other duties demand his service. The time devoted to friends is precious time, but it should never be excessive.

The second caution possibly does not greatly pertain to the city pastor, but one in a smaller community must exercise care in selecting personal friends in his own church and community. Many people are all too ready to hurl into the face of the minister the accusation that he has "pets" or favorites. He must do everyhing within discretion to prevent such a hurtful attitude among any of his people. He should lead them to feel that he is as much a friend to all as to any particular one. Much of the danger from this criticism, however, is removed if the minister is careful of the time he spends with his friends. Ordinarily, he will do well to have most of his closest friends outside of his own community.

Though the minister should have close personal friends, he should be known as a friend to all men. He should be a friend even to his enemies. In this he has the example, as well as the command, of his Master. He should be the sinner's friend, the very best friend the sinner has, other than Christ. A sympathetic, friendly attitude toward the sinner will go much further toward winning him than cold denunciation. Sin must be denounced, but not the sinner. The minister should be a friend to those who are in legal trouble, to those who are perplexed by doubts, and to those who are crushed by problems.

Those who are in need or in sorrow especially require his friendship. He should be very discreet, however, in his dealings with those in need. He is likely to be trespassed upon in this matter. Ordinarily he should not give directly, but indirectly. If he must give directly, he should do so with discretion. The gift should be only a means to an end and not an end in itself. The spiritual need even of the poverty-stricken may be greater than the material need.

And those in sorrow, how they do need the sympathy and friendship of the true minister of Christ! One of the greatest opportunities ever afforded the minister to enter into the hearts of people and to win them permanently for the Lord comes when sorrow has befallen them—sorrow caused by calamity, by children or other relatives having gone wrong, or by the death of loved ones. It is in such times as these that the heart of the minister is really found out.

The minister should never betray the secrets entrusted to him as a friend. When the downfallen have taken him to be their friend and have unburdened their hearts to him, he is a traitor if he betrays them. Much can be learned in this respect from the Salvation Army workers.

In his attempt to be a friend to mankind the minister need not think that it is necessary for him to be a "good fellow" or a "hail-fellow-well-met." This will lower him in the opinion of self-respecting, thoughtful people. Not only does he lower himself, but he also dishonors his Lord. Such cheap tactics are not consistent with the dignity of an ambassador of the King of kings.

How, then, shall the minister cause people to look on him as a friend? Three things are essential. He must, first of all, be *sympathetic*. This must not be a shallow matter, or merely a formal expression from the lips. The formal expression will not be greatly needed if there is real compassion of heart. People can tell if it is real. It should be the true minister's constant prayer that the Lord may bless him with Christ-like compassion for needy men.

A second essential is *understanding*. The minister must know men and convince them that he understands their conditions and needs. In addition to all that he himself can do, he will constantly need the direction of the Holy

Spirit in this as in other matters. Deep understanding of men and their problems comes with deep spiritual insight.

A third essential is *love*. As stressed elsewhere in this volume, the minister must love men with a consuming passion. The one common characteristic of all the truly great preachers of all ages, so far as one is able to judge, is that they really burned with love for men. Those who love their Lord most also love their fellow man most. The minister who loves men will have no difficulty in winning their confidential friendship.

Napoleon paid eloquent tribute to Jesus, declaring that Alexander, Cæsar, Charlemagne, and himself founded empires. "Upon what," he asked, "did the creations of our genius rest?" Answering his own question, the great Napoleon said, "On force." He continued, "Jesus Christ alone founded his empire on love; and at this hour millions would die for Him."

Christ built His kingdom on love. Likewise must His servant build on love.

8. The Minister and His Wife

Possibly no more worthy and less honored group of people can be found anywhere than ministers' wives. As a whole they are exceedingly heroic and self-sacrificial. Since the day the prophet declared, "How beautiful upon the mountains are the feet of him that bringeth good tidings, that publisheth peace; that bringeth good tidings of good, that publisheth salvation; that saith unto Zion, Thy God reigneth!" there have been people to rise up to praise the ministry; but few, indeed, have ever taken the trouble to honor the minister's wife, whom God has used so effectively in helping to make the ministry what it has been. It is wise, therefore, that attention be given to the subject. "The Minister's Wife."

It is fortunate, I think, when the minister enters his calling, or knows that he is going to enter it, before he marries. It is especially fortunate for his wife. Then she knows, or should know, what to expect of life. She does not marry a man of some other calling, thinking that her life will be thrown into another channel, only to be disappointed later. Tragic situations have been known to arise after a husband engaged in some business or profession has turned to the ministry. It is fortunate for the husband that his marriage come after his decision to enter the ministry, because he can be more careful how "he falls in love." In other words, if he be wise, he will seek a help-meet who at least has potential qualities suitable to a minister's wife. There is hardly any excuse for failure at this point. He will know full well that a girl who is worldly and concerned only about things secular or social is not likely to become a good companion for him. He has another advantage when the girl he takes to himself knows that she is marrying a minister, for he can be more assured that he will have her sympathetic co-operation in his work. This is no small matter.

The unmarried minister is wise to pray that God direct him in this exceedingly important duty and privilege—for it is both—of selecting a wife. Too much is involved for him to do otherwise. Many tragic unions might have been prevented by following this rule. There is no relation which the ambassador of the King of kings may enter which is unimportant, certainly not the relation of marriage. The matrimonial bonds, in sacredness and importance, are second only to one's union with God in Christ.

I

Certain personal qualities are extremely important, if not absolutely essential, to the making of a good wife for a minister. The first and most essential quality is Christian character and ideals. It is nothing short of tragedy if the minister's wife is not a real Christian. She will be the constant object of scrutiny by the feminine element of the community. If she is what she ought to be, she will readily become an example. She will be admired and followed. But if she is not what she ought to be in character and reputation, then woe to the minister. The success of his ministry is doomed.

The pastor of a certain church was loved by his people and admired for his good preaching. In every respect except one the people were greatly pleased with him. His wife, the neighbors reported, "made his home a hell." The church soon felt itself compelled to get rid of him.

Of all people in the world, it is the minister who most needs common sense and tact, and next to him, or equally with him, his wife needs these priceless virtues. They are among her most valuable qualities to her husband and to the church. By only a word, a look, or move that is out of place she may do irreparable harm. The blessing of these qualities, however, is not merely preventive; it is positive in the fullest sense. Only a simple word, look, or move at the proper time may produce results the invaluable good of which it will take all eternity to unfold. The records in heaven alone will reveal the countless times the thoughtful wife of a minister has tactfully inserted words that prevented the floodgates of trouble from being flung wide open. Blessed are those ministers whose wives have common sense and tact!

Another quality which the minister's wife should possess is refinement. She should be neat, ladylike, and free from vanity. Reasonable personal pride is justifiable, and pride with respect to her home is commendable, but she should never allow herself to manifest self-esteem or haughtiness.

If she does, she not only destroys all her influence for doing good, but she also becomes an encumbrance to her husband. She should always be agreeable, but not in a weak, acquiescent sense. These qualities will not be sufficient to make her refined, however, unless she adds "to temperance patience." It will be one of her most needed virtues. It is doubtful that Job's patience far excelled that needed by the average minister's wife. Through all the vexations that come her way, however, it will be imperative that she possess her soul in patience.

She will need education, both general and specific. It will be her duty to associate with educated people as well as with others. To demand the respect of these people she will need to be on the average, or above, in educational training. The nature of her work will also call for specific training. I am persuaded that there is great need for a special course of training for ministers' wives only. Many of the things which otherwise they have to learn by the trial and error method, or experience, or perhaps never learn but should know, could be taught in such a course as this. Such a suggestion may seem superfluous, but since the wife plays the part she does in the making or breaking of a minister I think it highly justifiable. Other specific training should also be added, such as that afforded by a course in religious education. It would not be a waste of her time to take a course in homiletics, since, after all, it is usually she who does more than any other person living, even including the homiletics professor, to shape—and keep in shape—her husband's manner of preaching. Blessed is that preacher whose wife is an able and sympathetic critic.

To her many other personal qualities a final but by no means insignificant one should be added. The minister's wife will need to possess the fine art of thriftiness or frugality. Though the preacher should be exceedingly careful about his business relations, the fact remains that all too frequently he is not. It is a blessing indeed to such a man if his wife is able to direct these affairs for him. The minister's home must be kept neat and attractive, the family must be becomingly dressed, the children must be educated, the minister must be a liberal giver to all religious and charitable causes. These and numerous other demands are made on his meager salary. The wife probably has the more difficult rôle and often deserves the credit for making this salary cover all obligations.

The minister's wife who does not possess all these personal qualities should make it her diligent pursuit to cultivate them as rapidly as possible. To a great degree the success of her husband's ministry depends on her attainment in this respect.

II

And what should the minister do for his wife? This is a question which deserves but receives all too little consideration. In the first place, it is his divine obligation to provide for her in a material way. Paul was talking to a young preacher when he said, "But if any provide not for his own, and specially for those of his own house, he has denied the faith and is worse than an infidel." * Certainly Timothy was expected to apply this statement to himself as well as to others. It is not expected that the minister should attempt to keep his wife in luxury; in fact, he should not, but he should keep her in comfort and enable her to keep herself and her home respectable.

The minister is obligated to protect his wife from avaricious and voracious church organizations and the like which attempt to devour her time and strength. If she is the type of person mentioned earlier in this paper her services will be demanded for the presidency, or some other office, in practically every organization of the church, especially organizations of women and children. The wise pastor will protect his wife from these unjust demands.

He should co-operate with her in rearing the children. Too frequently practically all the responsibility in this important matter is cast on the mother. The children, especially boys, need a father. They need him not only as a disciplinarian, but also as guide and comrade.

The minister should take his wife into partnership in all his plans, especially those which affect her, and practically all of them do affect her in some way and to some degree. This is a matter of simple respect, a matter made obligatory by the bonds of wedlock. If the wife is what she ought to be, it will be to his own advantage to consult with her.

In his busy daily rush all too frequently the minister

* I Tim. 5:8.

is forgetful of the fact that his wife deserves a reasonable amount of pleasure. He is forgetful because he finds diversion in outside relations and contacts which his wife does not have. He should never allow the drive of his daily ministry to prevent his giving a reasonable amount of time and thought to the pleasure of his wife and family.

A final and very serious obligation of the husband is that he should never give his wife any grounds for doubting him, especially in his relations with other women. A certain pastor is a very strong preacher and leader, and is, if possible, overdiligent in pastoral work. There is, however, one serious charge against him. His wife is living a life of mental torture because of her fears concerning his faithfulness. He is markedly too attentive to other women. Frequently he has left her waiting at home while he drove other women in his car. He has been known to fill his car with other women until there was not room left for his wife, and then to take them to a convention or the like while his wife remained at home. Yet he strongly avows his undying love and seeks to justify his conduct. Such a condition is not right and is worthy only of the strongest condemnation.

III

It is in order now to ask the question, What is the obligation of the minister's wife to her husband? In the first place, she should be interested in his work. If she finds herself not interested she should search her own heart to know the reason. As the wife of God's called servant, her life also should be devoted to His cause.

She owes it to her husband to make helpful criticisms, but never before others or when he is under tension. The easiest course, perhaps, is to "let well enough alone." This is not the way, however, to real growth. It is the wife's privilege and duty to help the minister grow in every way that is needful. Her love and ambition for him should lead her to give serious thought to this point.

The minister's wife may help protect her husband from feminine snares. Usually more readily than her husband, she can detect the subtle ambitions of an evil woman. She should be on guard in this respect. Sometimes she will prefer to remain at home rather than visit with her husband. Sometimes the need for rest or the lack of physical strength may justify her remaining at home, but for the sake of the reputation of her husband and for the sake of the cause he represents she will forget herself and go when circumstances demand that she should. When it comes to the protection of one's reputation an ounce of prevention is worth more than a pound of cure.

Another important obligation of the minister's wife will be to keep confidences. It is a haven of blessing to the husband if he is assured that he can discuss all matters of his work with his wife, knowing that she will never allow the secrets of their discussions to leak to anybody else. She should live on a plane far above that of a gossip.

The minister's wife can be a blessing to her husband by manifesting a sense of humor. He will often be sorely

vexed and worried in spite of all that he can do to prevent
it. He will come into first-hand contact with persons and
problems that will leave him bewildered at times, but if
his wife will make wise use of the "saving sense of humor" she will be as a steady veteran to a battle-scared
soldier.

What are the responsibilities of the minister's wife to
the church? The answer to this question is of greatest
importance. There are people and organizations that will
make her a scapegoat for their failures if possible. There
is no valid reason why she should put any more time into
the work of the church than any other woman who is a
member. In fact, there is less reason that she should. She
serves through her husband. Her life is devoted to making it possible for her husband to serve better. Her work
is, therefore, unique—different from that of any other
woman in the church. Thus, in a true sense, every day of
her life is devoted to the welfare of the church.

Usually she should make an iron-clad rule as binding as
the law of the Medes and Persians not to hold any offices
in the church. Many reasons could be offered in favor of
this rule. If she holds an office it is likely to be the cause
of dissatisfaction, for no officer can please everybody. If
she accepts one office, there is a tendency for the people
to think that she ought to be willing to take many offices,
and if she refuses they are offended. When she holds an
office it is likely to prevent her having as great knowledge
of the work as a whole as she should have. Her many
duties prevent her giving the necessary time to an office.

When she holds office, it usually causes a decreased interest on the part of others, who if they held the offices themselves would be more active. Finally, it is the duty of the minister's wife to train leaders. To do this she will push them forward to positions of leadership. She will actually be leading, but she will do her leading through the leaders. She will take her position as an adviser and guide. Her life will be a power behind the organizations and activities.

In the opening of this chapter it was suggested that the life of the minister's wife is one of self-sacrifice. In God's faultless direction of the affairs of His kingdom no sacrifice is ever made in His name that does not bring an abundant reward. Much of the reward to the minister's wife will come even in this world. She will have rejoicing after a time as she sees the results of her patient labor. Then surely her treasures will be great in the life to come.

Yes, her life may be one of self-effacement, self-denial, and self-sacrifice. She may be in the background while others receive the honor for the success of her labors. In fact, she may seem only to be keeping "the home fires burning" while her husband goes out to battle, but be assured, "as his part is that goeth down to the battle, so shall his part be that tarrieth by the stuff: they shall part alike."*†

*I Sam. 30:24.
† Every minister's wife, and, indeed, every married minister, should read *The Pastor's Wife,* by Carolyn P. Blackwood, The Westminster Press, 1951.

9. The Minister and the Age

A pastor once complained to the writer about an effort of a member of his church to make him a chauffeur, or rather a free taxi driver, for he was furnishing the car. The writer was called on a Saturday night, though he was to have four services the next day, to assist in making a decision about undertaker, embalming, and other details of funeral arrangements for a member of a family that was not even connected with his church. It was at least three o'clock Sunday morning before he could get home for needed rest, preceding the day's exacting duties.

The above are but examples of the many things which the average minister today is called upon to do. The demands of these times are multitudinous. They are so many that it is imperative for this reason alone that he decide what is rightly demanded of him and decline, or ignore, all the rest.

I

That which is wrongly demanded of the preacher may roughly be divided into two classes, the wrong from the standpoint of morals, waste of time or loss of influence, and the wrong because it is unreasonable and unjust. It is almost unbelievable, were it not so common, that men would seek deliberately to lead the minister into what is wrong morally. Stock promoters and the like are anxious to use the name of some minister in order that they may blind the eyes of the people. So various are their schemes that the minister must constantly be on guard lest he be trapped. Demands for visitation or association are also made that will, if accepted, mean the loss of influence. Demands for excessive attendance and addresses at clubs, societies, fraternities and dinners, if they do not lead to moral wrong or loss of influence, lead to extreme loss of time.

There are other unjust and unreasonable demands. It is unreasonable to demand of the preacher that he be perfect in every respect. The public needs to be made to realize, after all, that the minister is but a man, a man of like physical being and temptation as themselves. This is not an excuse for wrong-doing on the minister's part, but a plea for fairness.

It is unreasonable that the minister close his mouth on the great moral issues of the day. These issues, such as temperance, sex problems, and political corruption, all affect man's relation to God. They are essentially the business of the preacher as God's messenger. He can declare the fundamental teachings of the Word on such vital issues as righteousness in government without himself engaging in politics or stooping to the level of the politician. He should always be above politics and petty wrong-doings of political parties or even of individuals.

Once he has lowered himself to engage in such practices he has lost his power as God's prophet.

Another unreasonable and unjust demand made of many preachers of this age is that they preach only about the beautiful, and the pleasant to hear. They are never to mention sin or its result, or even to be very emphatic about the way of salvation. A deacon was heard to ask a certain very prominent pastor, "Why don't you preach like that?" The pastor replied, "If I were to preach that kind of sermon you people would fire me." The reference was to a certain sermon to which they both had listened, and which dealt with some of the fundamental issues of our faith.

II

It must be granted, however, that some of the demands made upon the minister by this age are just. The demand that he be sterling in character is not half so much a demand of the people as it is of the God whom he represents. Paul in his letter to the Romans, according to J. B. Phillips' translation of the New Testament Epistles, entitled *Letters to Young Churches,* says: "Let us be Christ's men from head to foot, and give no chances to the flesh to have its fling." *

The minister is engaged in the business of character building. It will be poor workmanship indeed if he is not able to exhibit in himself an example of what he is trying to build in others: "Called nobodies, we must be in the

* Romans 13:14.

public eye," says Paul.* It is right that leadership be demanded of the minister in this as well as in every age. God's ambassadors ought to be leaders. The fact that they must deal with "principalities and powers," not merely with flesh and blood, calls for greater ability than any other field of endeavor. Certain things are essential to the development of leadership ability, as, good training, scholarship, and ability to be agreeable with people. To these qualities should be added one other of importance, possibly of the greatest importance, namely, good judgment. This business-mad age will not tolerate the evidence of poor judgment. Many other shortcomings will be overlooked, but not this. Good judgment, of course, means that one must have the ability to think and to come to the right conclusions. It means also that he must be able to carry out his conclusions without defeating the proper ends.

The question of major importance to every minister is, or should be, What shall the minister bring to the age— intellectually, humanly, spiritually?

What shall the minister bring to the age intellectually? I would say, first of all, wisdom. If any person needs wisdom the Christian minister is that person. Certainly the wide-awake minister will feel moved to make Solomon's petition his own daily prayer: "Give therefore thy servant an understanding heart."

The minister should know himself, his fellow man and God. Certainly he can never know any to the fullest degree, but his knowledge should constantly increase. The

* II Cor. 6:9 (Phillips).

better he knows himself, the better he should know his fellow man. No public person will ever be as successful as he might otherwise be if he does not really know men.

Mention has already been made of the increasing demand on the minister of this age that he possess real scholarship.

A caution should always be kept in mind by the minister, and that is that all his intellectual attainment have an end, which end is not self. To be worth while it must be translated into that which will meet the spiritual needs of those whom he serves. Too frequently, increased intellectuality means decreased interest in the people. A preacher once told the writer that he found himself caring less and less for association with people, and desiring more and more to seclude himself in study. This tendency must be guarded against, for if the minister loses his grip on the people he loses all possibility of further helping them. For one to lose his interest *in* people inevitably means that he will lose his grip *on* them.

What shall the minister bring to the age humanly? He should bring a *refined self*. He should be genteel in manners and conduct. He should be clean and neat. One of the finest virtues he can develop is friendliness or neighborliness. In every way he should do his best to develop a well-rounded personality, one that is both winsome and compelling. He should also train himself to have a proper appreciation of the value of personality as found in others. He should not only appreciate its value, but also do his utmost to lead others into the fullest development of their personalities.

That which the minister should bring to the age spiritually is the most important of all. By word of mouth and by example of life he should lead the world to have a sense of the reality of God. To do this he must first have had a personal experience with God through faith in Christ. He must also know God in daily communion.

He should bring to the age a sense of the primacy of Christ. His life should be completely dominated by Christ. It must be his ambition and daily prayer to live so close to Christ in everyday experience that his fellow man may always be able to see the radiancy and beauty of Christ in him.

He should give to the world a sense of the reality of sin, of the tragedy of lives engulfed in sin, of the wreckage caused by sin, of the fate of lives given over to sin, and of the revelation at Calvary of the horror of sin. That minister who fails at this point has no message to give. If there is no sin there is no need of a Saviour. If the world is not convinced of its helplessness and ruin in sin it, in turn, will not be convinced that it has any need of the Redeemer.

The minister should bring to the world a sense of the reality of redemption from sin in and through the Son of God, the Christ of the Cross. This is the heart of the Gospel he is to preach. He is a physician for human woes —a physician for the chief human woe—and his only and all-sufficient remedy is the Christ of the Cross.

To do all the above the minister must have a profound conviction of the verity of the Scriptures, and an indomitable faith in the triumphant Christ. He must believe that

> Jesus shall reign where'er the sun
> Doth his successive journeys run;
> His kingdom stretch from shore to shore
> Till moons shall wax and wane no more.*

There is much discussion in some circles whether the minister will be able to continue to hold his place as an interpreter and reformer. Many people are expressing fear, some the hope, that the day of the pulpit's widespread influence is forever gone. But is it? It is a fact that in some places this is true. Almost invariably, however, these are places in which some "wolf in sheep's clothing" has been found out, or else where someone so liberal that he has lost his message is bringing shame to the cause. This class of preachers is negligible compared to that great majority of true ministers of Christ who yet wield a mighty influence for righteousness. The pulpit cannot wane in power so long as the ministers are true prophets of God. It is contrary not only to history, but also to reason, to think that God would permit such a condition to come to pass. In fact, one takes heart that there is promise of strengthening leadership in the pulpit in the days shortly ahead. There is a definite and widespread tendency, on the part of young ministers as well as older ones, to return to the Bible—to the bedrock of

* "Jesus Shall Reign," Isaac Watts.

divine revelation, to the ageless teachings of the Word. In proportion as this takes place the leadership of the pulpit will increase in authority and effectiveness.

If the pulpit is to demonstrate new power of leadership what shall be its program? It must be evangelistic, but shall it be intensive or extensive evangelism? It must be both, with major emphasis on the intensive. In fact, the best way to inaugurate a successful program of extensive evangelism is to begin a program of intensive evangelism. The evangelistic effort should go deep. It should reach the individual and change him to the depths of his being. When this is done, those who have been truly evangelized will become evangelistic themselves. The great reproach against the church of today is the fact that too much of its evangelistic effort has been a surface matter. It has failed to reach the vital parts of men's lives. Church rolls have been cluttered with the names of people who have never experienced the regenerating power of Christ in their lives. When "the swelling of Jordan" comes, they are not able to stand. Many have fallen by the wayside. Their lives, instead of being a blessing, have become a hindrance to the cause. Such a condition is deplorable, but it can be prevented by the right type of evangelism.

To place major emphasis on intensive evangelism does not mean that the importance of extensive or mass evangelism shall be overlooked. In fact, as our evangelistic efforts become more thoroughly intensive, they will automatically become more generally extensive. When persons are genuinely evangelized they burn with zeal to make the message of life and joy known to others both near and far. A thoroughly regenerated church is always a strongly missionary church.

The discussion of extensive evangelism naturally leads to an estimation of the ideal of the so-called "Christianization of the social order." Is the major business of the minister of today to give his best effort toward the creation of ideal legislation, the encouragement of better housing programs, and the improvement of general social conditions, or is there something else that should claim his chief attention? Certainly the true minister is interested in such things, but if he makes them his chief concern, with the hope of Christianizing the social order, he is bound for disillusionment. The only effective way to make this world better is to Christianize the individual. The regulations of the Kingdom of God cannot be made to work successfully where the souls of men are given over to the ways of sin. To this fact the present world chaos gives unlimited evidence.

It is to be wondered if Christians—even the best of Christians—did not put too much confidence, for example, during the days of Prohibition, in the strength of the law alone to make men sober and good. This is possibly one reason the Eighteenth Amendment was finally repealed. We too often forget that only the transforming power of Christ is able to make men good and sober. The only way really to improve men, communities, and even nations, is to change men's hearts. The Gospel of Christ is the only and all-sufficient remedy, for it alone "is the power of God unto salvation to everyone that believeth." The true minister will preach the whole Gospel, including its emphasis on personal redemption and its stress on righteous living, for both are included. He will be a prophet of God, not merely a social welfare worker.

There is a challenge as well as revelation in the following quotation, which, although printed several years ago, is still timely:

The world needs religion these days about as badly as it does money. I'm terribly disappointed in the world's clergy. I'd like to see the churchmen put aside secular topics and theological controversies to talk to the peoples of the world on the necessity for a rebirth of the old-fashioned faith that brought our forefathers safely through vastly more trying ordeals than the economic breakdown we are facing today. And I'd like to see the peoples of the world recalled from the shallow, wisecracking skepticism, now a modish affectation, to an honest belief in the helpfulness of prayer. The world needs to be re-educated in the old religion that faced its problems with faith and fortitude. As Dr. Henry van Dyke puts it: "The culture which leaves a man without a flag is only one degree less miserable than that which leaves him without a God." *

* Quoted by permission. From "Viewed By and Large," in the *Philadelphia Dispatch*.

10. The Minister and the World of Tomorrow

The question may appropriately be asked in this day of global revolution and unparalleled catastrophe, What will be the place of the Christian minister in the world of tomorrow?

There can be no denial that it is bound to be a different world. Modern war, with its carnage and high carnival of hell, has made a shambles of much of the earth. The world has been bled until it is almost anemic, laid waste until much of it is barren, pillaged until much of it is desolate, debt-ridden until it is almost bankrupt, bereaved and burdened until it is heartbroken.

Education may have to be modified. The old ways of living for personal gain alone, without regard to human welfare, must go. All of life should be on a different plane. Our whole social system needs reconditioning.

The late Senator John H. Bankhead, a member of the powerful Appropriations Committee of Congress that appropriated some two hundred billions of dollars for the World War II effort of this nation, and one of the best informed men in Washington, said a while before his death, to a gathering of his fellow townsmen in his home city, at which the writer was present, "Prepare yourselves for the future. Save your money. Pay your debts. These things we must do, for we are coming inevitably to a lower standard of living." As taxes and the cost of wars go higher, this prophecy threatens to be fulfilled.

In the coming new world will the minister of Jesus Christ be able to command a hearing? The answer to this question seems as simple as it is breath-taking. *The minister's place in the world of tomorrow will be determined to a large degree by what the minister says and does in the world of today.*

The history of the Christian ministry, like the history of the Christian Church, has been a succession of "highs" and "lows," with too many "lows" to make it pleasant reading at all times. It is cause for thanks that there have been the "highs." There were Peter and John and Paul, Origen and Athanasius and Gregory, Augustine and Anselm and Bernard, Aquinas and St. Francis of Assisi and Boniface, Luther and Calvin and Knox, Bunyan and Wesley and Whitefield, Spurgeon and Finney and Moody. Because of what these and others have done and said in the past, the Christian ministry, even in this day, maintains a phenomenal place of influence, all that has been said to the contrary notwithstanding. Of course, no one can know how much greater the influence of the ministry might have been now if in the past there had been in the pulpits no stammerers, equivocators, compromisers, cowards and peddlers of half-baked theories but only proclaimers of the eternal verities.

But it will do us little good to dwell entirely on the history of the past or the failure and successes of the present.

What we must do is to gird ourselves for the future. Two questions of great pertinence now arise: (1) How may this be done? (2) Will it be done?

Concerning the first question, the answer, to the present writer, seems clear and unmistakable. It is set forth in the other chapters of this discussion, especially in the chapter, "I Magnify My Office." If the ministry would make sure that it girds itself for tomorrow let it make sure of its Conversion, Conviction, Consecration, Courage, Constancy. In addition to faith that will not waver, three superior vitamin B's—Brains, and Brawn, and Blood—will be required. The minister of today must lead wisely, serve sacrificially, and preach prophetically, if he is to have the attention of men tomorrow.

The editor of *Fortune* was speaking for more people than himself when he said, as the clouds of World War II began to gather about us, "There is only one way out of the spiral. The way out is the sound of a voice, not our voice, but a voice coming from something not ourselves, in the existence of which we cannot disbelieve. It is the earthly task of the pastors to hear this voice, to cause us to hear it, and to tell us what it says. If they cannot hear it, or if they fail to tell us, we, as laymen, are utterly lost. Without it we are no more capable of saving the world than we were capable of creating it in the first place." *

What *Fortune's* editor was pleading for then must be given to the world now. If this is done the Christian ministry will come to an eminence of influence such as it

* *Fortune,* January, 1940.

has never known. The prophet of old based the proof of the inspiration of his message on the claim that time would validate it. "And when this cometh to pass, (lo, it will come,) then shall they know that a prophet hath been among them." * Again, time will prove whether the voice of the ministry of today is the voice of God.

The second question now moves into the focus of our observation, *Will the Christian ministry gird itself adequately to meet the future?* The problem as to how it may prepare itself to take the forefront of leadership tomorrow is not more perplexing than the question, Will it do so?

This much is certain, the Christian ministry despite all the determined forces set against it will have at least *a* place in the world of tomorrow. Let no one doubt this fact. It is based on certain affirmations of the Christian faith which are so well established as to be axiomatic. These are: First, there is a God, moral, intelligent, personal. Second, this God is immanent, as well as transcendent. He is not far-removed from our lives and the affairs of the world, but is Immanuel, God with us, desiring to have communion with men. He has to do with all men and is intimately concerned in all their affairs. Third, this God has never allowed the world to be utterly without His witness and directing voice. Throughout all ages, without exception, He has laid His hand again and again on somebody as His messenger. Fourth, this God has

* Ezekiel 33:33 (R. V.). See also Deuteronomy 18:21-22, and Jeremiah 28:9.

promised to continue to speak to men and to unfold His directive will to them.* Fifth, men who are called of God *will* speak for God. Ultimately, that prophet on whom God lays His hand *will* prophesy. The vision given through John the Revelator concerning the two witnesses in Revelation 11:7-11 may be taken as an assurance, it seems to the writer, that nothing can permanently overcome God's messengers. Their voices may be silenced in some places temporarily, as in the wickedness of Sodom or the bondage of Egypt, but "after three days and a half the spirit of life from God entered into them, and they stood upon their feet, and great fear fell upon them which saw them." God will not be left without witnesses. There can be no permanent blackout of His message. Even persecution, instead of hushing the prophet, simply challenges him.

Yes, the Christian ministry *will* have a place in the world of tomorrow, but what will be that place? *If certain signs mean anything, it should be a larger, more influential, more dynamic, more vital place than ever before.*

There are three important considerations which give cause for hope regarding the ministry in the new world of tomorrow. First, this disillusioned world is undoubtedly more able than ever before to realize its need for a message of certainty and authority. "The world," says Dr. W. O. Carver, "is more consciously lost than ever before." All

* John 14:26.

human panaceas and Utopias having fallen, and the wisdom and plans of those who have been in the place of political and social leadership having failed, and the amazing and almost incredible discoveries and developments of science having been frustrated, surely men ought to be prepared as perhaps never in the past to hear the voice of the man of God. Signs already multiply that there is foundation for this hope. The voice of the minister right now, it seems, gains more attention in some places than has been the case for several decades.

Newspapers seem to be giving more space than for some time to quoting from Christian leaders. Even more books of fiction are being based on Biblical history and more movies of a religious character are being produced than before. Challenge after challenge appears in editorials of national newspapers and periodicals to the ministry to point the way out of the present chaos. From the pen of David Lawrence comes a statement which may be taken as typical:

> But does not the crisis of today afford the very opportunity which the Church has been waiting for—something that makes it possible to turn the rank and file and the leaders once more to the simple principles which have come to us through two thousand years of human experience? Who then are the Captains and the Generals in the new army of Moral Force which must be mobilized here and abroad? They are the militant spokesmen of the Church who have given their days and nights to the task of elevating the human spirit.

May they sound the bugles that will call human hearts to action.

May they teach us the language of prayer which we have forgotten in our era of creature comforts.

May they tell us in homely terms of a simple faith how to ask Divine Providence to help us sacrifice and even suffer so that mankind may by its own regeneration destroy these new forms of idolatry and substitute therefore an unremitting worship of the merciful God before whom must stand, when the final Day of Reckoning comes, all the mortal dictators of human destiny, the leaders and the led, the rich and the poor, the oppressors and the oppressed.*

What a challenge the disillusioned world, ripe for a message from God, presents to the minister today. How much greater the challenge is likely to be when the disillusionment of this chaotic day is fully wrought out! No wonder a prominent preacher exclaims: "How one does wish he could preach today."

Many missions-minded men and women [said a seminary in one of its pamphlets during World War II] regard the conflict now raging throughout the world as an indefinite *parenthesis* between yesterday's laying of spiritual foundations and tomorrow's challenge for Kingdom expansion. Within this parenthesis of time is an opportunity to prepare for a task so *huge* that God's assistance in wrestling with it is being sought even today when peace seems so far off!

When at last the world lays down its arms and takes a good look at the pitiable fragments that remain, then will

* Editorial in the *United States News*. Quoted by permission.

material man know his impotence and *spiritual man* be summoned from the four corners of the earth. World call! Divine opportunity!

A second consideration which gives cause for hope even in this present darkness regarding the place of the Christian ministry in the world of tomorrow is the fact that the exigencies of the times will soon eliminate all but the true and bona fide ministers of God, so that those who are left will be the kind who will validate themselves. This is a consequential matter. The chief hurt and handicap of the ministry has come, in the past, not from the opposition without, but from the false prophet and the spiritual weakling within. Both of these elements are marked for elimination in the purging fires of these times. Only the genuine prophets, possessed of great spiritual fortitude, will be able to stand. But how they will stand and have always stood! Burnings at the stake, inquisitions, and concentration camps have never stopped them. Even while dying, they pray such prayers as to reverberate down through the centuries. Tyndale died at the stake and was burned to ashes on October 6, 1536, but his dying breath was a fervent prayer, "Lord, open the King of England's eyes." Still the echo of that prayer rolls on.

Greater heroism has never been manifested than that of intrepid missionaries who at the hazard of their lives have stayed on at their posts of duty regardless of every warning and of every human tendency to flee. The consequence of their suffering to the natives among whom they were serving must have meant a profounder respect

for the missionary and belief in the integrity and super-
natural quality of the Gospel. This has already resulted,
in turn, in the opening of doors of opportunity for effective witnessing, except where the onrush of Communism
has temporarily—as this writer believes—hindered it.

Hope for a more influential place of the Christian ministry in the days before us may be based also on the fact
that there has been a definite and almost universal shift
of theological thought and preaching from barren liberalism to the great central truths of the Christian faith.
At no place is the shift more apparent than among the
acknowledged leaders of the Christian bodies of the world.
It is not smart any longer to be liberal; it is archaic. In
the past the children of the world cried for spiritual
bread, but were often given a stone. Consequently the
hungry gradually turned away. But it is becoming different now. We have been forced back to the Foundations.
Men have learned that social diatribes will not suffice
when men's hearts are bad, that an absolute criterion is
imperative, that "men must be governed by God or they
will be ruled by tyrants." We begin to see now that not
the law of evolution but of devolution seems to be the
natural tendency of man. The halcyon days of confidence
in the supposed escalator rise of mankind have departed.
Now thoughtful men know that something is so radically
wrong with man that a radical remedy will be required.

In a revealing interview, Chaplain Merrit Williams,
who was aboard the aircraft carrier *Wasp* when it was
sunk November 2, 1942, said, "Religion, to be of impor-

tance to the sailor or soldier, must have something convincing to say about God." The chaplain might properly be corrected: Religion, to have any value to *anybody,* must have something convincing to say about God. Liberalism failed (not because it was not concerned for man's good) but because it forgot this essential fact. Now that, through the crucible of world suffering, the fact has been rediscovered, we may rightly expect to see a new day of great preaching begin to dawn. May God hasten the dawn!

There is a warning in the following words of Jowett which ought not be forgotten:

> If sin has become a commonplace, our preaching has become a plaything. If we do not feel its horrors, we shall lose the startling clarion of the watchman. There will be no urgency in our speech, no vehemence, no sense of imperious haste. If we think lightly of the disease, we shall loiter on the way to the physician. If we do not feel the heat of the consuming and destructive presence, we shall not labor, with undivided zeal, to pluck our fellow men as brands from the burning. If our sense of sin is lax, we may find in that laxity one of the causes of ineffective preaching.*

Revival fires are already being kindled in many places. Larger crowds than have ever been recorded are reported to be attending certain evangelistic efforts. A youth movement in evangelism has a world program under way. Although communistic aggression has closed the door to the Gospel in some places—we pray only temporarily—

* From sermon "Secrets of Effective Preaching," in *Apostolic Optimism,* Harper & Brothers, 1930, p. 268.

other doors have been opened wide, and thousands are being led through them to Christ. All the major and many of the smaller evangelical communions, including some of the more staid and liturgical ones, have begun to project great evangelistic campaigns. Many leaders feel that the world may be on the very threshold of a great spiritual awakening. This is the day for great preaching and great expectancy.

As faithful exponents of the Eternal Gospel, ministers in the days ahead will remember that "God is *well able* to transform men into servants who are satisfactory," * and that "nothing you do for him is ever lost or ever wasted." ** Consumed, then, with a passion for the lost, convinced of the adequacy of the Gospel of the Lord Jesus Christ, compelled by a sense of the urgency of their mission, and constrained irresistibly by the love of Christ, these ambassadors, commissioned with the one genuine and abiding message of reconciliation, will keep on declaring to a fallen world, "Make your peace with God," until this message is no longer needed.

* Romans 14:4 (J. B. Phillips translation).
** I Cor. 15:58, *ibid.*

11. The Minister and His Study

Many of our preachers are studying too little. Some of them know it and most of their people know it. Both the preachers and the people are to blame for it: the preachers because of lack of the drive and discipline required, and the people, because either they do not understand the need or do not sense their responsibility to help.

"The preacher," it has been said, "is not a gushing geyser of good advice, but an announcer of good news." But if he is to be more than a gushing geyser of good advice, there is a price to pay.

"Preaching that costs nothing," it is warned, "accomplishes nothing." The cost which effective preaching exacts may take many forms, and one of those is vigorous study. Altogether too little is said about this either in books directed to preachers or in counsel given to churches. Most preachers in this day, to be sure, do agree that study is an essential part of their work, but there is far too little information available to the busy pastor as to how he should use his study, and there is a grave lack of information for churches as to their part in helping the pastor to make wisest use of the study. Indeed, almost nothing is ever said to our churches concerning their crucial responsibility in this whole matter. Many members of churches seem to think that a minister ought to be engaged entirely in visitation and organizational work without time for study and that he really needs little or no time for study. Yet lay people quite commonly complain that their pulpits have little of real depth, freshness, and importance to say; but they never stop long enough to reason why this is so.

The famed preacher, J. H. Jowett, recalls a remark made to him once by an eminently successful attorney. According to Jowett, when this attorney was complimented for his brilliant effectiveness in the courts he commented, "Cases are won in chambers." The lawyer was saying that it was not so much his work in the courtroom or in public that brought success as it was his study in his office.

It is too easy to assume college and seminary training alone is sufficient to carry a preacher through life without further study. The truth is that this has only prepared him to begin to study. A wise pastor will likely study harder after his formal training than before.

But why should a preacher study? First, because he is so directed in the Bible. Paul in writing to Timothy urges, "Study to show yourself approved unto God, a workman that needeth not to be ashamed." In I Peter the elders are enjoined to "feed the flock of God." Little feeding of the flock is possible, unless the minister is continually feeding his own mind and soul.

But proper study obviously calls for a special place for study. Though there has been a commendable awakening to this need, there are yet apparently many of our churches which have not seen the necessity, for their own good and the strengthening of their pulpits, to create a suitable place either in the preacher's home or in the church for a "study." Such a place ought to be reasonably comfortable, but more than this, it should afford privacy and a place for the assembling and best use of books and other materials the preacher needs for his work. Almost no one can be expected to accomplish much in a study where his privacy is not preserved.

Incidentally, well instructed and thoughtful church people do not make a practice of telephoning or otherwise interrupting the preacher, except in emergencies, in the hours he is supposed to be engaged in study.

When should the preacher study?

At least a half day five days out of every week. It is preferable that the hours for study be the freshest hours of the morning. If other times must be used, they should be times when there will be an opportunity of extended and uninterrupted work.

How should the preacher use his study? The answer to this question must be determined by the capacities and nature of each man but for everyone the first use, and perhaps the most important, is for prayer, Bible reading, and communion with God. This, of course, will be for the refreshing of one's own soul, without regard to the preparation of any sermon in particular. Such hours of communion and meditation can be as the burning bush to Moses, the cave to Elijah, the hired house to Paul, or Patmos to John.

A second use of the study will be for specialized training of the mind and broadening of one's knowledge.
Deep, thorough research in one book of the Bible after
another should be a part of one's study. In following a
plan which calls for such study, one comes onto treasures
of inestimable worth. Obviously, in this study, one is
well advised to have certain aids at hand; such as, various
translations of the Bible, a concordance, a good dictionary
of the Bible, and several of the better commentaries. These
are as important to the minister as the hammer and the
saw to the carpenter. One may, in addition, wish also to
have on hand some of the better books of sermons on
books of the Bible, but these should be used only after
one has done his own research. Then the further light
found in a good book of sermons may help to correct one's
own work or to suggest a better plan of treatment.

Beyond specialized study of books of the Bible, the
preacher should also study great doctrinal themes of the
Bible, endeavoring to trace these themes throughout the
Scriptures, as well as to study theological books upon
them. A study of personalities, periods, or the historic
events unfolded in the Bible will also be richly rewarding.
A knowledge of the background and history of the books
of the Bible is virtually essential of course for proper
understanding of the message given. In addition to the
above studies, one needs to broaden his field of general
knowledge in order to know the world in which men live
and the nature and thinking of men. One should, therefore, set apart some of his study time for informing him-

self in the fields of history, literature, sociology, psychology, and like studies. Beyond all this, one should go on to study of the life and work of the church and methods which may be used to carry on the work most effectively. He will especially be concerned about such great themes as evangelism and missions. "How to do it" books, on these subjects, as well as books of inspiration are desirable.

All of the above adds up to two important considerations:

1. The pastor who applies himself and fulfills his demanding task properly must study. He must study deeply and broadly. He must keep on studying as long as he would keep on effectively serving.

2. The churches, many of which complain about the "diet" they get from the pulpits could do a great deal more to encourage and assist pastors in their study. The demands of our present church programs, and the busy rush of modern life combine to keep the pastor from doing the kind of study he ought. Only by the understanding and assistance of the people as well as by the strong resolution of the preacher will this be done.

Admittedly, study is not everything. The minister must be God's man among the people and a shepherd of souls. Visitation of the people, especially of the sick and of others in particular need, and the work of soul-winning never cease. These with the regular services and organizational meetings which the pastor must attend and the vast amount of personal counseling he may be called on to do will take all of the time a pastor can give them. They should not, and must not, however, be allowed to take his whole time. Both the pastor and the people do well to remember this.

In insisting upon the necessity of careful, continuous, and exacting study on the part of the minister, it is not implied that such study is a substitute for the work of the Holy Spirit in the life of the minister. Indeed, with all the preparation possible, the preacher can at best be only sounding brass and a tinkling cymbal unless he is filled with both the love of God and the power of the Spirit. But if the New Testament is to be our guide, then it seems obvious that the Holy Spirit is more pleased to use one who gives adequate time for preparation than one who is busy here and there all the time and merely presumes on the Holy Spirit to fill his mouth and use him when he enters the pulpit. The latter comes dangerously near being the type described by Halford Luccock when he speaks of the pulpit that is reduced to the ghastly predicament of living on its wits. "And wits," he says, "no matter how sharp, are a vain thing for conveying God's saving word to the heart and the mind. The preacher who depends upon his wits, either real or imaginary, on tricks or verbal novelties, or the child's play of exploding little homiletical fire crackers, has really filed a petition in bankruptcy as a Herald of God."

12. The Grandeur and Gravity of the Ministry

Some people have suggested that ministers, like many others, have feet of clay. The view is altogether too conservative! The minister, again like others, is wholly made of clay! Says the great Apostle Paul, "We have this treasure in *earthen* vessels."

The New Testament scholar, A. T. Robertson, once wrote a book entitled, *The Glory of the Ministry.* He based his thought on the writing of Paul, as revealed in II Corinthians 2:14-7:10. In this volume, Dr. Robertson attempted to gather up and interpret Paul's vast conception of the exalted privilege and significance of the Christian ministry, especially as the apostle had portrayed it in this Corinthian letter.

There is perhaps no passage anywhere in literature which more majestically and masterfully sets forth the loftiness and labor, the cost and consequence of the work of one called to the ministry of Christ than does this statement by Paul. A careful examination of the passage under consideration will reveal that in it the apostle not only tells of the grandeur of the ministry, but also speaks of its gravity. There are always these two sides to this high calling. These two contrasting elements, indeed, are inescapable both in the biblical presentation of the ministry and in the history of the ministry at its best. It is but natural, therefore, that these elements are found intermingled in the thought of Paul.

Both the grandeur and the gravity of the ministry are manifested in the *ordinariness of the minister himself, on the one hand, and in the glory, on the other hand, of the ministry of Christ itself.*

With at least three telling expressions, Paul points up in this Corinthian passage the humbling fact of the ordinariness and even the "earthiness" of men called to the ministry, an ordinariness common to all. In doing this, he declares, first, that ministers are *"earthen vessels"* (4:7); secondly, that they are *"mortal flesh"* (3:11); and thirdly, that they are *"servants"* or slaves (4:5).

No matter what our background, culture, position, or training as ministers, we cannot get away from these humbling, if not sometimes humiliating, realities. Whether dressed in flowing academic regalia or the bishop's colorful gown or in an impressive business suit, one is still only an earthen vessel. "Our sufficiency" always, as Paul insists, "is of God." (3:5). Unless the Spirit takes the "vessel" that we naturally are and fills it and works through it, we are, therefore, bound to be of little use. Neither our brilliance nor our learning, our impressiveness of personality nor our well-groomed physique, our position nor our possessions will at last make us effective for the good of the souls of men unless God works in us and through us. The only time the transforming *word* of God is really *heard* from the pulpit or the life-changing *presence* of God is actually *felt* in a service is the blessed occasion when God chooses to speak through the man or to work in him.

The warning words of Christ to His disciples, "Without me you can do nothing," continue to echo down across the centuries. We do well, indeed, to remember that we are "earthen vessels." We do well also to remember that we are "mortal flesh." The "humanness," the "fleshliness," as well as the perishable nature of the minister are apparent. That is, they are apparent to others if not to him, for some men are hard to convince. "Don't argue with a fool," it is warned, "for the people listening may not know which one the fool is."

Ministers bear in themselves, for example, the same capacity not only for diseases and other physical disabilities as do others, but also the same tendency to temptation. There are weaknesses to be overcome and impulses to be put to death. Ministers live in a house of flesh which they must understand. They reckon with the *physical man,* the depths of whose possible degradation they must not underestimate nor the heights of whose reach they dare not overlook.

Henry Ward Beecher, when once asked why so many pastorates were short, replied "The mercy of God." Though some of us seem to feel we are essential to a given work, it is always amazing, if not actually deflating to our own *egos,* to learn how well the Lord can get along there without us.

An old lady declared in disgust, "The ministers that

the congregation can stand, can't stand the congregation." Too often this is so, and it is so because we are all so human.

More dangerous than his eccentricities, oddities, and other natural weaknesses, however, is the minister's lack, at any time, of guardedness against the unworthy impulses and subtle lusts that rise within him or may take advantage of him from without. Some of the most tragic chapters in the life of the church have been written as a consequence of this lack.

A young minister of remarkable personality and gift, who was destined, in the judgment of many who knew him, to rise soon to one of the top leadership posts in his denomination, suddenly fell victim to the plot of an evil couple. The couple apparently used drugs in coffee to trap the preacher, but possibly his own lack of adequate guardedness helped also to trap him and to lead him into a situation which, in a few swift moments, wrecked his whole active ministry. The shock and grief caused to his family, congregation, friends and the whole Christian community from this tragedy, was incalculable. Such an instance enforces the truth that the minister must ever keep before him the biblical reminder that he is "flesh," even "mortal flesh," and valiantly and determinedly keep this flesh under his mastery. "I keep under my body," Paul said, "and bring it under subjection; lest that by any means, when I have preached to others, I myself should be a castaway." (I Corinthians 9:27)

The minister's ordinariness and consequent need of

humility — not posed but real — is evidenced also by the fact that he is a "servant." In II Corinthians 4:5, Paul uses *doulos,* the word meaning "slave," to characterize the minister. This is the lowest term for "servant" of four used in the New Testament.

Paul always looked upon himself as only a servant or slave of the Lord Jesus Christ. "It is possible" someone has warned, "to become terribly self-centered in the ministry." One is all the more likely to slip into this deplorable state if he ever forgets that he is just a servant.

Men never rise higher in the ministry than when they seek truly to serve rather than to be served. The church has but one rightful Lord. It needs no little "tin gods." Ministers are called not to become "officials" but servants. If they are true to their calling they will long to see their Master and not themselves glorified.

Spurgeon, in one of his great sermons on "The Name of Jesus," ended his message thus, "Jesus! Jesus! Jesus! Let my name perish, but let His name last forever." That is every minister's proper prayer.

Alongside the truth of the ordinariness of the minister, we rejoice to say, stands the glorious reality, however, of the grandeur of the ministry. The grandeur of no position is greater than that of the witness and service of Christ. That is the other side of the coin and it is lustrous indeed!

In II Corinthians Paul refers to the privileged task of bearing the Gospel as a "treasure" (4:7). He sees the work of the minister, moreover, as a "sweet savior" among men (2:16). Still more impressively he declares the whole work of the ambassador of Christ to be that of a ministry of "reconciliation" (5:18) like the work of an ambassador to a foreign land. The minister then holds the high office of ambassador, of representative of the Courts of Heaven here on earth. It is little wonder, therefore, that Paul declared, "I magnify my office." He, of course, did not magnify himself, for he could not forget his unworthiness and ordinariness; but how he did magnify his office!

One would be hard-pressed to find conceptions more thrilling and expressive than those Paul used to reveal the glory and the grandeur of the ministry. To him this ministry was truly a "treasure." The Williams translation uses the word "jewel" for "treasure." The Gospel itself and the witness that makes this glorious message effective among men, in truth, are a "jewel" — a jewel of greatest worth. Who could estimate what the value of the preaching of the Gospel and of serving the Christ has been to the ages? And who could over-estimate the worth of the "treasure" committed to us in the privilege of being witnesses and servants of Christ — albeit we hold this "treasure in earthen vessels?"

DATE DUE

APR 0 7 1998			